2.50

P9-EDQ-761

THE IMPERTINENCES OF
BROTHER ANONYMOUS

The Impertinences of Brother Anonymous (Frère Untel) is Volume Two of a series on the FRENCH CANADIAN RENAISSANCE.

Other volumes in this series

Pierre Laporte, *The True Face of Duplessis*, 1960, 1970.

Paul Sauriol, *The Nationalization of Electric Power*, 1962.

Hugh Bingham Myers, *The Quebec Revolution*, 1964, 1972.

Jean-Paul Desbiens, *For Pity's Sake : The Return of Brother Anonymous*, 1965.

Books on related topics

Raymond Tanghe, *Laurier : Architect of Canadian Unity*, 1966, 1971.

Claude Jasmin, *Ethel and the Terrorist*, 1965.

Jacques Hébert, *The Temple on the River*, 1968.

W. F. Mackey, *Bilingualism as a World Problem*, 1967.

W. J. Eccles, *Canadian Society during the French Regime*, 1968.

Howard Adams, *The Education of Canadians, 1800-1867*, 1968.

Casey Murrow, *Henri Bourassa and French-Canadian Nationalisim, 1896-1920 : Opposition to Empire*, 1968, 1972.

Anne Hébert, *The Torrent*, Forthcoming.

Jacques Ferron, *Cotnoir*, Forthcoming.

THE **IMPERTINENCES**

OF

BROTHER ANONYMOUS

Preface by ANDRÉ LAURENDEAU

Translation by

MIRIAM CHAPIN

HARVEST HOUSE, MONTREAL

Ninth Printing
1972

Copyright © Canada 1962, 1972 by Harvest House Limited ;
Library of Congress Catalogue Card Number 62-14443

Printed and bound in Canada

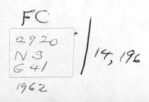

CONTENTS

EDITOR'S NOTE

Brother Anonymous is above all work of literature — an immaculate case of human creativity. By good fortune, although it was no accident, it was born in the Province of Quebec in this our Canada.

The relatively youthful teaching Brother, now identified as Pierre Jerome, writes with the rollicking keenness of a Molière, and the gleeful art of Heinrich Heine. The river of universal genius flows through his work. With Rabelais, the sixteenth century monk — precursor of that earlier renaissance he cries — 'There is also the body'.... "We have had enough of Quebec's Jansenist shudders."

Only incidentally do we report that this is a book about education, language, religious bureaucracy, and personal freedom. Through Brother Jerome's own history and the light which he casts on the fate of the people of Quebec, we learn more about life and work of a folk than could be adduced by an army of researchers with all the calculating ordnance they could muster. Erasmus-like he writes and struggles for reform from within the Church. While his book has not been "banned in Boston" or even placed on The Index, Brother Jerome himself has allegedly been sent off to Rome to further his theological studies. There is also a great shaking of wise heads about him that I don't understand, saying: "You know he won't be writing anything for a long time to come". Pierre Jerome will be missed in Quebec. But, not to divulge a secret, genius rarely occurs singly. Usually the same felicitous milieu creates three — four — five — a dozen. Awake Canadians, there are giants in the land!

There is a further reason why the issuance of the English language edition of Frère Untel *is timely. A Royal Commission on Education now sits in Quebec. To this august body Brother Anonymous has much to say. True, he betrays his classical background by making too tight a distinction between trade and profession, intellectual and physical labour. Yet, he does it in the interest of excellence, of the mastery in depth of subject matter by the teachers, so he is absolved.*

Brother Anonymous will also be present when the 2000 delegates of the 2nd Canadian Conference on Education meet in Montreal this March. For, give a little here, and take a little there, and they will find that they have a lot in common with him. I needn't elaborate. They will understand whose problem he refers to when he says: "Living joual means rock'n roll, hot dogs, parties, running around in cars. All our civilization is joual."

And again, this book will do much to destroy the myth of the isolation of French Canada from European movements. The reader will be put in touch with Continental currents of thought — intellectual — social — religious — literary, and, he will be enriched. Tolstoi and Gorki, Sartre, Bergson and Péguy, Bernanos, Alain, Julian Huxley — here is the opening to democracy and liberalization of institutions in Quebec that the rest of Canada has allegedly been waiting for. There will be no turning back. The fresh air is doing its work. Let's welcome it! Of two major Canadian achievements in the Valley of the St. Lawrence since the War, the building of the Seaway and the writing of Brother Anonymous, the latter may prove to be the greater.

Finally, to those French Canadian friends — and there are many — who say that Les Insolences du Frère Untel *is untranslatable, I oppose the words of Gandhi. No linguist himself, he faced the problem of speaking to a subcontinent where scores of languages were spoken. As he said: "... in spite of having to communicate with them in English, I felt entirely at home. What barrier is there that love cannot break?'*

Maynard Gertler

January 1962

* * *

TO THE 1965 EDITION

With the fifth printing of this now-classical Canadian work, a new word from the author seemed in place. Brother Anonymous (Frère Untel) has had so much to do with hastening educational reform in Quebec and with the stirring of self-consciousness in all branches of its cultural and social life that one naturally refers to him for current advice. He has obliged with a brief new communication.

The recent death of Miriam Chapin who accomplished what was solemnly described as "impossible" in translating the highly idiomatic FRERE UNTEL left us with a sad task of securing a translator for the author's new "dedication". Fortunately, Montreal is the home of the talented novelist Gwethalyn Graham whose knowledge of the French language is informed by association with her Québecois neighbours and by girlhood education in Switzerland. It is her excellent translation which appears in this edition.

Meanwhile, Brother Anonymous asked whether I like his new text. Like Nature he is "seldom mild", and ordinarily his little gems summon all one's emotion and intellect to the alarm. With great restraint I replied:

"Yes, I do like your introduction, although our experience has been different, so that I feel the critical urgency of stressing common humanity — even in Canada...."

DEDICATION

A dedication for this kind of book is all wrong, and to dedicate it to two men makes it worse. Usually a man dedicates a work to someone he wants to honour, to an old schoolmaster or a young mistress. But to dedicate a book of impertinences to anybody is beyond understanding.

Why to Michael Golaneck? He is a Ukrainian born in Canada, a nurse at the Lake Edward Sanitarium; he was for a long time a patient at Laval Hospital, where he left a lung. I knew him at the sanitarium, where I lost the best six years of my youth. Maybe that explains my combative instincts. Michael is a gentle, modest man, even though as a good Russian he talks a lot about sending people to stay in Ungava and about machine-gunning his hopeless cases. He has one passion and that is justice. He can hardly read and write, which has never kept him from thinking straight. My father can't read and write either, but he is no less intelligent for that. Here in Quebec we are only the second generation of literates. We still read very little and write more or less badly.

Michael and I spent many hours talking over "social questions," as the snobs would say. He has some ideas which he thinks are "communist," because he knows nothing about Christianity; actually Michael is what I would call an agnostic. He doesn't believe in the resurrection of the flesh; instead he believes that animals will end up talking Latin — that's his bug. Even so I'm sure he will enter the Kingdom of Heaven ahead of me — no great accomplishment, for my place in the Kingdom will probably be in Row Q. He has a naturally Christian heart, as somebody said, Tertullian or Bossuet, I haven't the time to look it up. One night he gave me, almost word for word, St. Basil's diatribe against the rich, though you can be sure he never read a word of St. Basil. "If you admit that these things have been given you by God, do you want God to be accused of injustice for having distributed his property so unfairly? Why are you wealthy while your brother has to beg, if not so that you may acquire merit by giving away your goods, while your brother wears the crown of patience? The bread that lies uneaten in your cupboard is the bread of the hungry, the coat hanging in your closet is the coat of the naked, the shoe lying unworn in your house belongs to the poor man going barefoot, the money that you hoard is the money of the destitute. Every time you fail to help, you commit an injustice."

I make no claim to honour Michael by dedicating this book to him — he is above all that. I talked to him of my plan to write it that summer; he said, in his hesitating way, "Even if you do publish your book, say to yourself that you are a worthless servant." I dedicate this book humbly to Michael Golaneck, in token of friendship.

Why to André Laurendeau? To dedicate a book to such a well-known man when one is only Brother Anonymous, could be the gesture of an ambitious man. But everything began because of him. When I first wrote to him, in October, 1959, it was a personal letter. It was he who decided to print it, it was he who picked the pseudonym under which I have been working ever since. He struck the first blow, without which nothing would have happened. Every time I met him after that, it was an event for me. Some may say I was a little carried away. I came from very far, both geographically and socially, being only a teaching Brother, a proletarian of the Holy Church (Quebec version).

In a certain sense, Laurendeau is a teacher. I believe he has done more to educate French Canadians than most of the certified teachers, more to give them a backbone than most politicians. That's a good reason to dedicate to him a book about teaching. So to André Laurendeau, in token of gratitude.

* * *

DEDICATION

TO THE 1965 EDITION

So it seems you are about to issue another edition of the *Impertinences* in English. I am somewhat astonished. This book was written in 1960 and that was twenty-five years ago, because nowadays each year counts for five. It is true that English Canadians are still living in 1760 so for them to find themselves catapulted into 1960 represents quite a jump.

In Quebec, the *Impertinences are a museum piece*. I ought to take myself in hand and publish something else before I tumble into history. I don't doubt that the sociologists of 1980 are going to have to explain the success of this little book as a sociological phenomenon to be treated with solemnity and lots of graphs and statistics.

It all began with a letter to André Laurendeau. It was a personal letter, not intended for publication. But it was published. Other letters followed, a dozen of them, each meant to be the last so far as I was concerned. The weeks went by, the holidays were upon us. Then, one day, a note from Jacques Hébert: the letters should be published, with some additions and some cuts — in short, a book must come out on September 6th. And it was already July 18th. Why the 6th of September? Because that year classes started on September 6th and the whole population had their noses buried in it. In what? The educational problem. Once that day is past, quoth Hébert at the Bastogne where we were dining together that 25th of July, 1960, everyone will return to his other problems and the schools will be back in their rut. Since then, every day is the day classes start. But I am anticipating.

Agreement is reached. The book is to be out September 6th. And it was. The little bark was launched on the stormy seas of public opinion for its confounded cruise, and me with it.

No one, publisher, author or the reading public expected such a reaction. The phenomenon can be explained, somewhat hesitantly and at least in part, as follows: for five or six years public opinion had been in a ferment over the problems of education, and crystallized around the *Impertinences* just as water crystallizes at 32° Fahrenheit.

Don't imagine that the *impertinences* are only concerned with scholastic problems, for in fact this booklet nails down the chief problems of French Canadian society — problems of language, teaching, the cultural and religious atmosphere. The author (myself) wanders innocently about with all the confidence of a man who isn't an expert on anything. Alice in a wonderland of sluice gates. Behind the sluice gates are backed up an immense reservoir of thought, impatience, and a desire to do something. It was the bursting point. One of my friends compared the situation of Quebec in 1965 to that of a newly born baby drawing his first independent breath of whom it is said, and I can well believe it, that it hurts. We French Canadians are taking our first breath as a nation conscious of its entity. We are emerging from "two black centuries of depression," as Canon Groulx says, quite rightly. Our young generation is the most nationalistic we have ever had, and we are orchestrating, as a nation, on every level, psychological, political, economic. And in two years there will be the rendez-vous of 1967.

Canada is a political reality but it is not a psychological reality. A strange country, decreed by men in defiance of geography, with its frail backbone of railway lines, inhabited by two non-contemporary peoples. What will become of it and its single maple leaf? You ought to be pondering the question, you people of English Canada.

The danger is that you will forget to really give it thought, while we will have made our choice on our own.

Publishers who translate French Canadian works are doing all they can to synchronize the clocks of Toronto and Montreal, but readers should not forget that the *Impertinences* belong to a quarter of a century ago.

Quebec, 16-2-65.   Brother Jean-Paul Desbiens

A SORT OF PREFACE

By dint of being often attacked and sometimes praised, a journalist grows less sensitive to other people's opinions. He has a tough hide, and yet —

I remember a letter that came to me last fall, following a rather bitter squib I had written on the language our young people speak. It was from a Brother, a humble Brother in a far-off region. There was in it a certain flair for expression, a nice turn of speech, that touched me. We published it. So was born Frère Untel.

Why baptize him Frère Untel? In the first place I didn't think for a second that he was a fraud. According to all the evidence, this man was a teacher, one of those who day after day puts his hand to the plough, who keeps the freshness of his purpose, but admits that the work is hard and the soil resistant. He was an anonymous Brother, the first to come out of the army of Brothers. He was a good spokesman, incarnating all that is best among them, the voice of all those who work in shadow and silence, those that we never hear. So he was Frère Untel, Brother So-and-so.

We have met twice since then. I can reassure the doubtful that here is a man of flesh and blood, a member of a certain community, assigned to a regular task in a Quebec town. He is an enthusiastic and simple man, with a taste for good food and witty talk. I think he loves his work, loves the boys he teaches, of whom he sometimes speaks harshly, and even the authorities who are the targets of his impertinent sallies. But his instinct makes him most at home with simple people, especially the old folks who have never come out of obscurity. I understood that better after I read his all too brief account of his origins. He has kept something of his naïveté, but he is pretty shrewd. He has suffered.

It seems to me the attitude that suits him best and lets him be most truly himself is that of an obedient son who still complains of the meagreness he feels in a too distant and ritualistic authority. Disappointment, though he feels it keenly, does not make him bitter; if he is sometimes flippant, he does not lose his reverence for the sacred. He has kept his good nature, as is easy to see in the portrait he sketches of himself. I hope he keeps his taste for reality and his clearsightedness now that he is launched on the sea of notoriety.

André LAURENDEAU

What a fool you are, Pastor Quixote, to fight these stinking lies with only the weapons of love and light and generosity, in order to rescue these poor galley slaves even if they stone you! For be sure they will stone you, if you break the chains of cowardice that bind them. But precisely because they will stone you, you must deliver them. To stone their liberator is the first use they will make of their liberty.

MIGUEL de UNAMUNO, The Life of Don Quixote and Sancho Panza.

WARNING

I work with the axe, though I don't like to. By temper-
ament I am rather delicate, and nostalgic about the past. I
enjoy Oka cheese and coffee laced with brandy. But in the
land of Quebec this is no time for delicacy. When everybody talks joual, it's no time to watch the fine points of
grammar. If a man is asleep in a house on fire, the
neighbours don't wake him up with Mozart's *Eine Kleine
Nachtmusik*. They yell at him, and if he still sleeps soundly,
they kick him out of bed.

The members of the French Canadian Academy and
the Royal Society will be wasting their time if they deplore
my extravagant language and my unseemly paragraphs.
I write with an axe. (Hi, what a metaphor! You're getting
incoherent, little Brother. That's terrible. You blame your
pupils for the like of that, and you think you can get away
with it?) I will not repeat it, that's how I write. Later on
we can split hairs when priests and cabinet ministers no
longer talk joual.

You see I have conquered once for all any temptation
toward perfectionism, which means preferring emptiness
to imperfection, trying to be angelic. You can't dirty your
hands if you haven't any. I am willing to accept temporary
solutions; my writing is not academic, it is an urge to action,
and every action is more or less dirty. Every action is
desperate.

To clear the ground is not to build, but we have to begin
by clearing away, and before that by demolishing what
was there. St. Léon Bloy declared he was an expert at
demolition. Fifty years later I take over from him, as a
lesser genius (it's proper for me to say that, but I don't

believe it) as is fitting in a country two and a half revolutions behind. By the American clock, we are at the time of the Middle Ages.

I will have none of any criticism of this work based only on its form. I don't despise form, but it is not enough. I know perfectly well that to be without form does not guarantee substance, I know that even what has substance will not last without form. But I reject such criticism because a writer falls back on form when he is too compromised, too wishy-washy, too tricky to go to the bottom of his subject. I write as well as I can, without trying to be a stylist. My texts are actions; I'm no tightrope walker.

To pretend that I think form is the most important part of my work would be cheating. The pharisees — and all human activity, including literary criticism, coddles its own pharisaism — are first of all formalists. When you tell them they are rotten, they reply they can't accept such language because it is too brutal. But to pick up an anglicism or some little mistake in a text which reeks of joual is not serious, however smart it may be. Only dishonest people can play the delicate critic on articles that discuss the religious atmosphere of French Canada. Such remarks on the tone of an article are a jesuit method of avoiding the real issues. An expensive psychiatrist might say here that I feel weak and want to protect myself cheaply on this question of form — he would be wrong. I am confident. I'm in good form.

PART I

Brother Anonymous
Demolishes

CHAPTER I

THE LANGUAGE OF
DEFEAT

> We are proud of being vanquished, we play
> and work as vanquished men. We laugh, we
> weep, we love, we write, we sing as the
> vanquished. All our moral and intellectual life
> can be explained by this single fact, that we
> are cowardly and dishonoured vanquished men.
>
> LEON BLOY

In October, 1959, André Laurendeau published a short column in *Le Devoir* in which he qualified the speech of French Canadian students as "joual talk." He, not I, invented the name. It was well chosen. The thing and the name are alike, both hateful. The word joual is a summary description of what it is like to talk joual, to say *joual* instead of *cheval*, horse. It is to talk as horses would talk if they had not long since plumped for the silence and the smile of Fernandel.

Our pupils talk joual, write joual, and don't want to talk or write any other way. Joual is their language. Things have gone so far that they can't even tell a mistake when it is shown them at pencil point. "The man what I talk to," "We are going to undress themselves," and the like do not bother them. In fact such expressions seem elegant to them. It is a little different when it comes to mistakes in spelling, and if a lack of agreement between noun and adjective or the omission of an *s* is pointed out, they can identify the error. But the vice is deeply rooted at the grammatical level, and on the level of pronunciation. Out of twenty pupils whose names you ask at the opening of school, not more than two or three will be comprehensible the first time. The others will have to repeat theirs. They say their names as if they were confessing a sin.

Joual is a boneless language. The consonants are all slurred, a little like the speech of Hawaiian dancers, according to the records I have heard. Oula-oula-oula-alao-alao-alao. They say *chu pas apable* for *je ne suis pas capable*. (I am not able.) I can't write joual down phonetically. It can't be fixed in writing for it is a decomposition, and only Edgar Poe could fix a decomposition. You know the story where he tells of the hypnotist who succeeded in freezing the decomposition of a corpse — it's a wonderful horror story.

Joual, this absence of language, is a symptom of our non-existence as French Canadians. No one can ever study language enough, for it is the home of all meanings. Our inability to assert ourselves, our refusal to accept the future, our obsession with the past, are all reflected in joual, our real language. Witness the abundance of negative turns of speech in our talk. Instead of saying that a woman is beautiful, we say she's not bad-looking; instead of saying that a pupil is intelligent, we say he's not stupid; instead of saying that we feel well, we say we're not too bad.

The day it appeared I read Laurendeau's comment to my class. My pupils realized that they spoke joual. One of them said, almost proudly, "We've founded a new language." They saw no need to change. "Everybody talks like us," they told me. Some said, "People would laugh at us if we talked differently from the others." One said — and it is a diabolical objection — "Why should we talk otherwise when everybody understands us?" It's not easy for a teacher, taken unaware, to answer this last proposition, which was made to me one afternoon.

Of course joual-speakers understand each other. But do you want to live your life among joual-speakers? As long as you want merely to chat about sports and the weather, as long as you talk only such crap, joual does very well. For primitives, a primitive language is good enough; animals get along with a few grunts. But if you want to attain to human speech, joual is not sufficient. You can make do with a board and some whitewash if you want to paint a barn, but finer tools are necessary for the Mona Lisa.

Now we approach the heart of the problem, which is a problem of civilization. Our pupils speak joual because they think joual, and they think joual because they live joual, like everybody around here. Living joual means rock'n roll, hot dogs, parties, running around in cars. All our civilization is joual. Efforts on the level of language don't accomplish anything, these competitions, campaigns for better French, congresses, all that stuff. We must act on the level of civilization, which is easy to say, but what can we do? What can a teacher, buried in his school, do to halt the decay? His efforts are ridiculous. Whatever he accomplishes is lost an hour later. From four o'clock on, he is in the wrong. The whole culture contradicts him, contradicts what he defends, tramples on what he preaches, makes fun of him. I am not old, I am not very peevish, I like teaching, and yet I despair of teaching French.

Will you say I'm going back to the days of the Flood if I recall Bergson's words on the need for a supra-consciousness? We live joual because our souls are impoverished, and so we speak it. I am convinced there is no substantial difference between the degradation of our language and the slackness of our attitude to the fundamental liberties which a *Maclean's* survey revealed in October, 1959. When our youth has surrendered those liberties, as they seem to have done in practice if not in theory — the word liberty is still respectable — they easily give up grammar. The apostles of democracy, like the apostles of good speech, appear like gentle madmen. Our people keep their admiration for machines and technique. They are impressed by nothing but money and luxury; the graces of syntax do not interest them. I flatter myself that I speak correct French — not elegant, but correct. My pupils nonetheless speak joual; I make no impression on them. Indeed I fancy that they sometimes do not understand me. To be understood, I often must have recourse to one or another joual expression. We speak two different languages, my class and I, and I am the only one who speaks both. What can we do? The whole French Canadian society is foundering. Our merchants show off their English company names, the billboards along our roads are all in English. We are a servile race; our loins were broken two hundred years ago, and it shows.

There are many signs of this. The Government offers evening courses through various organizations. The most popular are the English classes. Everyone wants to learn English; it is impossible to get enough. There is no question of organizing courses in French. Among the jouals, joual is good enough. We are a servile race, but what good does it do to perceive that? See clearly and die. It's a fine prospect, to be right and die of it.

Accounting is taught in English, with English textbooks, in the Catholic Province of Quebec, where the system of teaching is the best in the world. Heaven is the essential thing, not French. A man can be saved in joual.

Joseph Malègue says somewhere (I know where, but I don't want to appear pedantic — a genius can be modest) "In mortal danger men cut every tie, upset their lives and break off their careers, so that they may come to the sanitarium for two or three years. Anything rather than death, they say." Aren't we at that stage? When I think, if I think at all, I think of Liberty, but when I want to act, I do what I'm told to do. Only despotism acts. If we are to be cured, energetic measures are called for. The axe! We must work with the axe!

a) Absolute control of radio and television. Death penalty for using joual.

b) Destruction by the Provincial Police of all business signs in English or joual.

c) For two years, the right to shoot at sight any official, any cabinet minister, any professor, any priest, who utters a word of joual.

This is no time to fiddle around. But even so we would not be acting at the level of civilization. Shall we acknowledge a major crisis? Shall we take account of a mortal peril, and rouse ourselves to meet it? What price are we prepared to pay?

Advertising is a fact of our civilization; it is there that we must strike. We shall speak French when — and not before — it is smart to speak it and disgraceful to speak joual, when radio and especially television speak French. We shall speak it by imitation and snobbishness, by the power of the seduction of the beautiful and by science, when everyone on radio and television speaks French. Publicity is the great school of our day, and the man who reads the commercials is the great schoolmaster. Everything can be saved by controlling publicity.

Mgr. Gosselin said to me one day that our compatriots in the West need *Dupuis Frères* catalogues more than secondhand books or even textbooks. Our people will say *portière d'automobile* and not *porte de char* when the manufacturers and the advertisers say *portière*. They would not say "king size," if from the start they had heard *format géant*.

I hear talk of a Provincial Office of Linguistics. I am all for it. The language is public property and the State should protect it as such. It protects moose and trout, it protects the national parks, and it does well; those are all public property. The State ought to protect the language just as strictly. An idiom is as good as a moose; a word is worth as much as a trout.

The Quebec Government ought to require respect by law for the French language in the names of companies and in their advertising. I understand that manufacturers and big trading companies must at some time or other appear before the Government to be registered or be legally recognized. That's the time the Government should lie in wait for them. "Give yourselves French names, advertise in French, or we don't know you," it can say. Then we would have no more Thivierge Electric, or Chicoutimi Moving, or Turcotte Tire Service. If these two spheres, titles and advertising, were watched as closely as Laurentide Park, the language would be saved right there. But will the Government be realistic enough to do that? We can be practical and still lack realism; shall we ever have a Government that will not be satisfied to be practical, and so in the end be made a fool of, but that will be realistic? Who can estimate all the harm practical people have done us by lack of realism?

Society ought to support culture. Only the State has the legal and administrative power to be effective at the community level. We teachers have nothing, except that we have right on our side. That is such a little thing, good for nothing until you come to die. You think I am a trifle lugubrious?

You must not think that in trying to drive out joual we educators are trying to sterilize our Canadian French, to turn it willy-nilly into Parisian French. I subscribe with all my heart to this paragraph from our study program for the secondary schools, 1958: "During three and a half centuries French has been deeply tinged by the daily life of French Canada. We must nourish it from its European sources and follow its development in France, without neglecting the legitimate Canadian contribution or the adaptation which environment imposes on every language." As an obedient son of my father the Department of Public Instruction and my mother the School Commission, I am happy to declare that this paragraph is perfect; there is nothing in it to quarrel over. You see how good-natured I am. A good paragraph is a good paragraph. We teachers, we know Canada makes a legitimate contribution, we are not fussbudgets. Some day, God willing, we can take time to split hairs, but now the house is on fire. I don't mind if my pupils say *poudrerie* for snowstorm, I don't cut my throat when they debark from a bus or embark on a train, though strictly speaking those words should be used only of a ship. If I remember correctly, the Massey Report has some sensible things to say on this subject.

I shall always remember the countryman at Lake St. Jean whom I asked if the bus from the Lake and the one from Quebec met there according to the timetable. "My Brother, they meet bridle to bridle," he said. A juicy comparison like that would have delighted Montaigne, who liked nothing better than to speak the French of the Paris markets.

Here and now let me settle the account of one objection that is made against those who attack joual. In *Le Travailleur* of Worcester, Mass., someone complains: "Just at the moment when the old Anglo-Saxon myth of the French Canadian patois begins to weaken, our cousins in Quebec have found a picturesque substitute, joual. To speak joual or not to speak it is the new subject of debate among Quebec dilettantes. Never mind what impression Toronto, New York or Paris receive, so long as it can be proved that the language of Quebec is not French but joual. This battle is typical of French Canadian quarrels. On the north side of the 45th parallel they practice a fourth theological virtue, disparagement. Because the students of Montreal and Quebec do not speak academic French, they are accused of speaking joual."

I have no wish to write at length on this outburst; I

could keep going forever. I will only say that I don't give
a hoot what they say or don't say in Toronto. (First prize,
one week in Toronto; second prize, two weeks in Toronto;
third prize, three weeks in Toronto.) Do we speak joual,
yes or no? If we do, let's quit being ostriches, let's accept
the diagnosis and take the cure. We can't go from door to
door, we have to speak out in public. Dirty bird that won't
clean his nest because the neighbours might see him doing
it!

I had already published three or four letters in *Le
Devoir* in which I had expressed my views, and numerous
readers had been writing in during some five months, when
the matter of *O Canada* suddenly came up. There was a
fine rumpus. I had conceived the idea of asking my students
(11th year commercial) to write the first stanza of our
national anthem, later on I asked the 10th and 11th year in
science. The result of this inquiry was distressing beyond
all expectation. We expected some mistakes in spelling, but
we were really flabbergasted by what we got. Here are bits
of the joual version: *Au Canada, taire de nos ailleux*, for
O Canada, terre de nos aïeux (Land of our fathers). For
Ton front est ceint de fleurons glorieux (Thy brow is
wreathed with glorious flowers) we got *Ton front est sain,
ton front essaim, ton front est sein de flocons,* and several
other variations. *Et ta valeur de foi trempée* (thy valor
tempered by faith) came out *Et cavaleurs de froid trempé,
de voir trembler, de foie tremblay,* and so on. (They were
like the girl who sang "And laid him on the green," in The
Bonny Earl of Moray every time as "Lady Mondegreen.")

Laurendeau remarked, "No use getting angry. But might
we ask a few questions? *Taire de nos ailleux* makes nonsense, but could it have some hidden meaning? And *cavaleurs de foi tremblée*, could that mean us, cavaliers of shaky
faith maybe?"

I think that it was from that moment that the whole
teaching staff of the Province began to react. I had the

proof that the best platform from which to strike home to
all the Quebec teachers is not the little blue book called
Public Instruction, but *Le Devoir.* All the men teachers read
it, while nobody reads *L'Instruction publique* seriously.
That blue book is a kind of harem, where to be admitted
you have to be a sort of professional eunuch — the necessary eunuch.

I received by way of *Le Devoir* a letter from a woman
teacher blaming me for having made fun of my pupils before everybody instead of explaining to them "the beautiful
words of our national hymn." I told her, through the same
channel, that I had done that long before. "A normal
teacher," I went on, "has a normal reaction before igno-
rance as flagrant as that revealed by our experiment; he
wants to go to the root of the evil, the failure of understanding. So I then explained the first stanza to all the
students, and I mean to do the same thing with the second,
where it says 'Born of a proud race.' But I foresee that I
shall have some trouble to establish that we do come of
a proud race, so little pride remains to us."

The teacher's reaction is characteristic of the beleaguer-
ed mind. Gérard Pelletier noted this in *Cité Libre* one day.
(The things you do read, my dear little Brother, the things
you do read!) Whoever in Quebec makes it his business to
write anything beyond two and two makes four is a dirty
bird who-fouls-his-nest. In a town under siege, monolithism
is the fashion. Whoever does not think like all the rest
automatically takes on the guise of a paid spy, a fifth
columnist, a big bad wolf that the little girls must look out
for.

Just considering our weakness in French is not enough.
We must also consider the almost complete lack of any
civic or patriotic education in our schools for the past
twenty years, the incompetence and irresponsibility
of many of our teachers, the incompetence and irresponsibility of our Department of Public Instruction. But only

an anti-clerical would take our Department to task. So then we have the best system of education in the world. The *Jeunesse Ouvrière Catholique* report doesn't show that, but never mind. We are a hundred and fifty years ahead of all other countries as to the essential thing (which is Heaven), aren't we? The proof that all is well lies in the absence of any quarrels over the schools since 1867. Another proof is that the Council of Public Instruction meets only once in fifty-two years. The last meeting before this year's was in 1908, and then they met only to congratulate each other, promoting each other to sainthood. We have nightmare programs and incredible textbooks. Just take a look at Verhelst's *Essentials of Philosophy*, and see what a Belgian canon can accomplish when he undertakes to sweat out philosophy to the glory of God (evidently) and the salvation of souls (evidently).

My inquiry on *Au Canada* showed that there is no more patriotic education in the schools. I think it showed a few other things. I have proof now that almost everywhere in the Province they've begun to write and explain our national anthem. It's a beginning. And I also have the proof that I can reach the teachers through *Le Devoir*.

Good old *Devoir*, brotherly old *Devoir*, cheers! Cheers for good old Filion! They've been saying that you grow old and prudent. No matter, you struck a stout blow for freedom. And cheers for you, Laurendeau, so sensitive and human, and for all the staff of *Le Devoir*. How I would like to meet a bishop of whom I would want to say, Cheers, good old bishop! I don't say there aren't any, but I've never met one.

CHAPTER II

EDUCATION FOR HEAVEN

We talk joual, we live joual, we think joual. The smart guys will find a thousand explanations for that, the nice people will say it's better not to talk about it, the little female souls will say we mustn't hurt mama's feelings. Nevertheless the only possible explanation for this lamentable failure is that the system of education is a flop.

Take a look at history, my friend. When the Department was set up, a century ago, the object of the authorities was to dodge two perils, protestantism (permit me that word; it's awkward but it's clear) and anglicization. No fault to be found with that purpose; it was valiant and legitimate, but just the same, it was tricky. The aim was not to strive for a goal, it was to avoid a precipice. They knew where not to go but they hadn't fully decided where to head for. Our present discomfort began right there; the Department was a dodging machine, an escape tunnel. We have never succeeded in disposing of that inherited confusion, in getting out of that blind alley. Incompetence and irresponsibility are the bastards engendered at the beginning by Madam Confusion and her pimp Misdirection.

A typical result of this incompetence and irresponsibility is the public secondary course. Everything about it has been improvised, programs, textbooks, teachers. Public opinion demanded public secondary education. They were

sold the label, pasted on an empty bottle. The trouble was
not due to evil intentions, but to muddle and false starts.
They tried to play two tunes at once without ever making
up their minds what to play. For one thing, they wanted to
save the private secondary schools, considered the national
reserve for the priesthood, and for another thing they also
wanted to satisfy public opinion. The Department has been
busy and efficient on the institutional side, the classical
colleges; it has passed all too lightly over the academic
side, the public secondary schools. The proper solution
required that they should distinguish (notice how neatly
I use the imperfect subjunctive) once for all between these
functions. They chose to fiddle about and improvise.
Primary teachers were hoisted into the secondary schools
with no qualifications except their years of service in
the primary grades, with no training, no textbooks, no
programs.

The primary grades, where the real purpose of the
Department comes close to coinciding with the one they
proclaim, has long been the object of all its solicitude.
Things don't go too badly there. One sign of this solicitude
is that the Normal Schools for girls, which prepare the
majority of primary grade teachers, are numerous and
scattered all over the Province, while until recently there
were only two Normal Schools for men, one in Quebec
and one in Montreal. The teaching Brothers were expected
to fill the gaps.

Only by hard struggle have these teaching Brothers ex-
tracted permission to do a little improvising of their own,
to cook up a sort of boys' secondary course. If the Department had wanted to spoil any chance of setting up such a
course, it could hardly have acted any differently. The
academic side does not interest the Department. Mind you,
our faultfinding applies only to the present secondary
course. We would like nothing better than a real one.

The incompetence of the Department emerges clearly
from the mess of programs in which we flounder. Their

irresponsibility shows up in that, never being definitely committed to anything, they can always retreat, change things round, contradict themselves, while none of us can ever find out who is truly responsible. When a man is accountable only to God the Father who is in Heaven, he can afford to take a few liberties with temporal history. It is dangerous, but not everyone has the imagination to perceive that. We live in a surrealist world.

The educators — let's call them the professors — of the public secondary course are stuck in the middle of a nightmare. We are constantly threatened with changes in the programs and we have begun to realize what such a change means, what it implies in the way of improvisation. We know what it's like to follow a program and get the textbooks for it a year later, or even not at all, as was the case with philosophy this year. We know what it means to work without the least idea of how long the course is supposed to last. Try to imagine the state of mind of a teacher who prepares for a class with the expectation that the next year the course will be all upset. Bees are robbed of their honey as fast as they make it; our teachers are robbed of their preparation as fast as they write it. We perform our daily task without ever knowing where we are heading. Find out from the proper authorities, someone tells me. The proper authorities answer me this way: "This information is given by the Certificate Committee which publishes its decisions in the review *Public Instruction* when it deems this is appropriate." This when-it-deems-appropriate has a protective and paternalistic air, an air of saying, "Don't get worked up; your Father, who is in Quebec, knows that you have need of information and will give it to you at the right time, O man of little faith." And it is signed André Raymond or Roland Vinette.

We are big fat fools, we teachers in the public secondary. Trusting such promises, we take hope. We wait for the *L'Instruction publique*. It arrives. (If, if I were not Brother Anonymous, pious, pure, Marist, I would write the word you know twice over.) In the April, 1960 number Mr. Vinette signs a surrealist poem under the title, "Information and Policies."

He works hard to say nothing, he repeats himself, he is mysterious, not because he is stupid — we know he is competent and intelligent and fully capable of writing French — but by the policy imposed on him. It looks as if the officials wanted to mystify us. Apparently we don't need to understand. The Department is a machine so regimented, so centralized, that it is impossible to find anyone responsible for anything. Everything is filtered through veils. The bits of information that are passed out to us are so finely screened that you never know where you are going, if indeed you are going anywhere.

The exercise of authority in the Province of Quebec is the practice of witchcraft. In politics we have the Negro-King. * For everything else, we have the witchdoctors. They reign by virtue of the fear and mystery they wrap around themselves. The farther away they can keep themselves, the more mysterious they are, the more often things can fall on us suddenly, the better, for then events can appear to come directly from God-the-Father, like the thunder in the days before Franklin. From time to time an inspector, very secretly, after exacting a promise that we won't tell, gives us quite unofficially a hint of some change to come. In the end we are informed at the same time as our pupils.

It would be so much simpler to tell us what we are to do, where we are to go. Informed troops are so much more efficient than those who are always being taken by surprise. The atmosphere of conspiracy in which we live is demoralizing and troubles us all. Either the Department has a policy which it can avow, or it governs empirically. If it

* Laurendeau's theory that the real rulers of Quebec use a French Canadian to govern the Province as the colonial powers would use a Negro chieftain to govern his tribe.

has no policy, it proclaims its incompetence; if it conceals its policy for fear of having it criticized, it reveals its paternalism.

Why can't Mr. Vinette tell us plainly what he wants of us? His article is just about as limpid as the war discourses of the late Mackenzie King. Paragraph Two spoils Paragraph One, and vice versa. I think I gathered that henceforth the secondary course will be divided into three sections, not including the classical, whose status is not so clear. There will be a commercial section, and a scientific one, subdivided into science-mathematics and science-humanities. What is not clear is what is to be the result of this procedure. Are we or are we not moving toward the college system? Are we, yes or no, going to provide the Province with a complete public course leading to all the university courses?

I wish Mr. Vinette — you understand that I address myself to him simply as the official representative of the Department — would talk to us like this: "My children, beginning next September we shall have colleges at this place and that; from now on we shall distribute colleges according to certain principles. (We have decided on that, for we have vision, no matter what Gérard Pelletier * claims.) The textbooks have been chosen already and stocked in certain places. The programs will be more than simple copies of the Table of Contents. So begin to put them together, for you will need them in September. We promise you that a textbook approved in September will not be withdrawn in February, as happened this year because God-the-Father-in-Quebec did not have available in September all the information that he had available in February."

We would also love to have Mr. Vinette tell us what he means by expressions like "capacity to prolong their

* Editor of *La Presse*.

studies," "classify the pupils in the courses that are suited to them," "intellectual aptitudes," and the like. I'm not kidding. Neither is he. We know very well what all that means, but we can't make up our minds to say it openly: only 12 per cent of the population can aspire to university studies. The problem is to pick the good ones. But the problem of problems is something else again. We begin to feel a presentiment about it.

The official schedule calls for two hours a week of philosophy. In the twelfth grade the school year is thirty-six weeks long, exactly 179 days in 1959-60. So that year we were allowed seventy-two hours; in most classes we managed to take a hundred hours in all, three a week. That seems reasonable to me. During this time we are expected to teach a little logic, a little metaphysics, a little philosophy of science, a little sociology. Under one option, psychology may replace metaphysics. A little of this, a little of that, makes too much. I think metaphysics and psychology ought to be left out. Metaphysics is too hard for the students of the classical colleges, three years older than ours with five times the time. I know philosophy can't be taught without some metaphysics but it need not be systematic. Some notions underlying every philosophical statement are metaphysical. A good professor will occasionally bring in a metaphysical idea, and that should be enough.

The same thing is true of psychology. The first words of the philosophy course have to do with psychology. Some general considerations on human knowledge are prerequisites for any such course. In the definition of logic itself the question of intellectual ability comes up. At the start one must speak of science and art, or one doesn't get started. An able teacher will give a minimum of doctrine on the theory of knowledge and the structure of the human soul, and bring in other matters as he can. Logic, science and sociology remain; it is important to keep sociology in the program.

Kindly don't forget that we are a public school (my

colleagues know what that means) and we have only three hours a week for thirty-six weeks. One can't make a philosopher in nine months; all one can make is a baby, philosopher or not.

A critique of the sciences is or ought to be the principal part of the philosophy course in twelfth year science, for the students in these classes intend to take up scientific studies and careers. They urgently need some critical notions about science. Logic should be studied just enough to give point to such a critique. Our students are almost all scientists without knowing it. I can't refrain from saying something here about vocabulary. In French, *scientiste* is a derogatory term, duly set forth as such in the dictionary. A *scientiste* is a man who swears by the experimental sciences, who recognizes no way to truth except through experiments which can be recorded mathematically. Our students, like our journalists, translate the word "scientist" into French by *scientiste,* which is wrong. In French a scientist is a man of science, a *scientifique,* if one may use an adjective as a noun. Most French authors adopt this usage. So henceforth we shall say that Einstein was a *scientifique,* but Renan was only a *scientiste.*

The distribution of material prescribed by this year's official program is not bad. As a minimum, a critique of the sciences ought to cover facts or definitions, laws and theories. What is not so good is the manual. Under pretext that Simard's is too difficult, they give us Renoirte's *Elements of a Critique of Science and Cosmology.* Simard's work is perfect for what we want in a course on the critique of science; it contains a doctrinal section and a collection of the greatest scientific texts, as classic in their way as Bossuet's orations or extracts from Corneille. Emile Simard is a professor in the Faculty of Philosophy at Laval University. His only fault is that he isn't Belgian, but after all not everyone can be Belgian.

A textbook to suit our needs is just as desirable in sociology. However the one we had this year is tolerable on the whole. The students liked it very well and so did the teachers. To deprive our twelfth year students of these two subjects would be a great misfortune, for I know by experience that my pupils have found their most enlightening and stimulating, their newest notions in them. It's important to insert a few critical ideas on the experimental sciences into the docile brains of our young people. Most of them, I say it without contempt, are " telephoning Polynesians," to use Alain's formula. (St. Alain, pray for us.) They are enjoying a technical honeymoon, a case of love with science at first sight. No harm to season the brew in their heads with a bit of criticism.

Sociology is equally necessary. The textbook we have this year, Verdier's *Modern Problems, Christian Answers,* is well written, though it could do with a few changes. For instance it asserts in big letters that a good Catholic cannot be a good socialist (1956 Edition). Doubtless that still stands as far as France is concerned, but here in a communiqué dated 1953, the Hierarchy declared that a Catholic may enrol and even work in the ranks of a party said to be socialist. It is an example of the sort of adjustments which a good professor makes as he goes along. Verdier covers quickly the history of the labour question, and analyses the responses which have been made to that question: the socialist response, in the European version, and the marxist response. He gives in detail the only acceptable response, the Christian solution. There, roughly sketched, is the program we have to cover this year. I can assure you that it is an eye-opener to our students. And it is urgent that they do acknowledge these questions. Televising and telephoning barbarians, swaddled in technology, — so far they know only the comfort it gives — for them a jet plane is something wonderful, for they have never seen, even in the movies, that a jet may drop bombs.

It's often said that professors teach error and confuse the truth, doing a lot of harm in both cases. We have heard too that "all that can be taught may not deserve to be learned." We have one recourse, to shut up shop. Céline writes in his *Voyage to the End of the Night* (So then, my little Brother, you have read Céline? You read too much, and dirty books at that!) "We would have to close down the world for at least two or three generations if there were no more lies to tell. We would have nothing more to say, or next to nothing." I think we would have to shut up the Department for a couple of years at least, and send all the teaching staff to school.

The crisis in all teaching, and particularly in Quebec teaching is a crisis among teachers. They know nothing, and they know that badly. (It is not by saying amiable things like this that I am going to make friends and succeed in life.) Back to school, all of you. You have to go. For two years. After that, we'll reopen the shop.

I have been correcting the philosophy examinations. One question read like this: "When are two ideas contradictory?" Out of nine hundred papers, not thirty answered correctly. All, or almost all, happily mixed up contradiction and contrariety. Now salvation doesn't depend on knowing that distinction, but we have to teach it. If 90 per cent of our pupils don't know it, either we haven't taught it or we have taught it badly. There is one other possibility, that this distinction is beyond the comprehension of twelfth year commercial students.

Another question read thus: "When are two terms equivocal? Give an example." The question is badly put; it should not say two terms, but one. Why two? Why not 113, or as many as you like? Not only do the teachers need to be sent back to school, but even more the officials of the Department — all of them, and in a hurry.

A third question asked the student "to show that we are free." It is highly imprudent to ask our Quebec youth to show that they are free. What if they did? In fact, they don't. They show only that they can repeat docilely what they think somebody wants them to say. Then they switch to talking about God and the Saviour and original sin. Most of the papers I corrected mobilized Revelations and God to show that they were free, evidently with Heaven and Hell in the background. If most of our pupils in all parts of the Province marshal these thoughts in their exams, it is because they have been stuffed with them. Philosophy is taught like the Catechism. The good Brothers, the good Sisters, the good lay teachers, imagine that a boy is a follower of Voltaire if he doesn't moralize. No middle ground exists, temporal and spiritual are confounded, in concubinage. Do you sleep content in your tomb, Constantine? And do you, Maria Chapdelaine with your voices? "The third voice, loudest of all, rose in the silence, the voice of the land of Quebec, half song of woman, half sermon of priest." I have heard in fancy this third voice of Maria, this voice of sentimentality and morality. That's the one that prevails among us, the little song of our entrails and the big song of the seven capital sins.

No one can go to work on a philosophy textbook, or even take the time to consider the program, unless he is more or less sure that something will come of it. Will there be a twelfth year next fall? Will there be a philosophy course? Is any serious work merely a vain effort? The confusion is so overpowering, the atmosphere of conspiracy so stifling, that no one dares undertake anything. The future in this area is so uncertain that a man lives as if awaiting the Second Coming. Programs are shaken up every two years, courses every six months. What shall we do? We are demoralized in one way by too harsh controls, by the uncertainty of the future in another. The wisest among us wait passively for the ukases of the beloved Department. The smart ones go into business, the printers print, the conspirators conspire, and everybody improvises.

All is for the worst in the worst of all possible worlds, you think. Oh no, Madame la Marquise, everything goes very well. Just comfort yourself with this editorial in the March, 1960 issue of our little blue *Public Instruction* review, entitled—and the title is a program itself—"For the child, for the adolescent, for the future...." They don't stint themselves. "The educators now have at hand the most varied means and those best adapted to present conditions. Our teacher training institutes admirably prepare numerous candidates, both men and women, for the teaching profession. Our working personnel can acquire new skills and complete their training by taking graduate courses. So we are all better prepared to accomplish our daily task, but our work will be truly efficient only if we know how to educate the man of tomorrow by developing the spirit, the intelligence, and the heart of the child of today. There must be growth, the child and the adolescent at all stages must feel that he is developing according to his own abilities. He is not a simple figure in a table of statistics, but a qualitative value for the school and later for the trade group, the profession, the society in general..." and so on and so on.

I am soft hearted, you know. I don't want to hurt anybody. Still, we must close down the Department. Let's give all the officials all the medals there are, not forgetting the one for Agricultural Merit. Let's create some special ones, such as one for Solemn Mediocrity. Let's give them all a comfortable and well-paid retirement and send them home to their mamas. That would be a lot cheaper than paying them to complicate our lives the way they do now. For there's one sure thing, the Department has given evidence of its incompetence and irresponsibility a hundred times over.

I cull the following from a letter sent me by Mr. Jacques Tremblay after my piece about the teachers' Great Fear came out in *Le Devoir*:

Fear is the keystone of the System, fear is what delays its disintegration after History has definitely condemned it. The System is one of mediaeval privilege, and as a corollary of that, of social injustice. It is a System of complicity between the clerics and the powerful, and so of holy irresponsibility; of sanctimonious angelism and so of arrogant incompetence; of proud dogmatism and so of obscurantism. What we find in the Department of Public Instruction is nothing but the reflection, perhaps the caricature, of our world.

Incompetence: the title of Bishop, or a nomination "at the pleasure of the Lieutenant-governor in Council" is all the diploma required to become supreme judge in matters of education. A man may have only a seventh year certificate or none at all and still be named "at the pleasure of the Lieutenant-governor in Council" Superintendent of Public Instruction. Merely by virtue of being a priest, a man is qualified to "watch over the good and efficient pedagogical organization of a normal school, to control (?) the teaching in it, and to direct the moral, intellectual and religious training of its students." Being "minister of a cult or member of a religious corporation" can take the place of any diploma or teacher's certificate. The principle of incompetence is set down in black and white in the Law of Public Instruction and in the Regulations of the Catholic Committee. It should be easy to line up a hundred instances to show how arrogant this incompetence can be.

Irresponsibility: no official of the Department of Public Instruction is elected by the people, and there is no possible democratic recourse whatever against any decision of the Department.

Social Injustice: it is instructive to see with what timidity and what "wise prudence" the authorities consider the problem of democratizing education, by way of free tuition, when we know that the poor, 90 per cent of Quebec's population make up less than 30 per cent of the university population.

CHAPTER III

PURITY THROUGH
STERILIZATION

In the paths where no one has trodden, dare
to step.

In the channels where no one has thought,
dare to think.

LANZA DEL VASTO

The failure of our system of teaching is the reflection
of a failure, or at any rate a paralysis, of thought itself.
Nobody in French Canada dares think — at least nobody
dares think out loud. The lack of any serious discussion
in the Province brands us in the most unforgivable way.
As talking to oneself is the beginning of madness, it's clear
that to spend one's time thinking, necessarily alone, is to
come close to madness. French Canada's tragedy is a tragedy of communication.

What we practice here is purity through sterilization,
orthodoxy through silence, security through dull repetition.
We imagine there is only one way to go straight, and that
is never to set out; one way never to make mistakes and
that is never to experiment; one way not to get lost and
that is to stay asleep. We have invented a sure way to fight
caterpillars — to cut down the trees.

We must grasp this failure of our thinking at its most sensitive point, at the heart of French Canada. There, at the very heart, let us study a clinical case, the Faculty of Philosophy. I said before that I am not writing for the finicky; I am going so far as to talk about philosophy, which is for everybody. You'll hear the man in the street saying that philosophy is no concern of his. Pardon me, sir, it does concern you. We worry a lot about radio-active fallout, but we pay no attention to philosophic fallout. Yet we are continually being sprinkled with philosophy. Mr. K. gives us our daily doses of Marxism through the press. Everybody is concerned with philosophy.

Fourteen million Russians stew in Siberia in the name of a certain philosophy. Six million Jews were gassed in the name of another. Philosophy always catches up with men, whether they think about it or not — maybe above all if they don't think about it. It is everybody's business and everybody must consider it. They say that it is nothing but a collection of cloudy principles, a paradise for jokers. But some day it will be your mother, your friend, your wife who will be liquidated in the name of some philosophy or other that you have let spread out of control. In *Time* August 1st, 1960, a full page is given over to the biologist Julian Huxley, who states tranquilly that God is a hypothesis and we can get along without Him. *Time* is read by at least two million people every week. This same Huxley spoke to us on *Radio Canada* not long ago. Philosophy concerns us all.

I studied in the Faculty of Philosophy at Laval University — I'm not complacent about that. It's no great thing to brag of. Jacques Tremblay and Brother Louis-Gregory, who helped bring this book to birth, studied there too. Those who say the Faculty of Philosophy produces only conformists are wrong. So far as my experience goes, I knew admirable men there, hard workers, sincere, intellectually honest. They made a deep impression on me, and I have never stopped being interested in the subject.

Just because I am interested in philosophy, I must examine it here. The fault of which I accuse the Laval Faculty of Philosophy, the fault that sums up all my grievances, is that it has no roots. I have the impression that the men who work there, either because they don't see clearly or they want to play safe, refuse to shoulder a great part of their real responsibilities. They have forsaken contemporary man and shut themselves away, under all sorts of pretexts, in a closed, protected, delightful universe, where they know very well they won't have to give an account of themselves to anyone unless to Parmenides or Al Farabi. They forget that History's bills always catch up with its debtors in the end. As Léon Bloy said, "You can't escape the cramps of failure's colic."

Some of Laval's philosophy professors seem to take pride in not writing anything. Their pretext is that writing makes thought too materialistic. Apparently that is one of the reasons why Jesus wrote nothing. It is true that their master, Mr. St. Thomas Aquinas, wrote a very great deal. Precisely so, what Thomas wrote is enough for them. They are satisfied to comment on his writings, when they are not commenting on the commentaries, the cube root of St. Thomas. If they write nothing, or write so badly that they might as well have written nothing, we must conclude that according to St. Thomas they are not good masters. He wrote this: "God, like a good master took care to leave us two perfect works to complete our education, the two divine books, Genesis and the Testament. Genesis contains as many excellent chapters as there are creatures." The great Thomas, let us note, was in perfect harmony with the Creation. He was the biggest YES ever uttered by a Christian. He said YES to everything, giving a wide welcome to the luxuriant Creation of God. Every creature, he said, is an excellent chapter which speaks to us of our Father who is in Heaven (not our Father in Quebec, contrary to what I said somewhere). Every creature that runs, from the woodlouse to Claude-Henri Grignon*, taking in Julia Richer** on the way.

During our period of study in the Faculty of Philosophy, courses that had anything to do with contemporary problems and the realities of here and now were very rare. Our professors never managed to marry the universal principles they flirted with to life. While we were taking our course, education was going through a crisis, with forums, discussion panels, student strikes, and the whole works. Not a treacherous word of enlightenment on such affairs ever made its way up Ste. Famille St. where our Sophie posed in the charming harmless gestures of her daily metaphysical round, the little trollop.

From time to time someone might pretend to duel a little with Bertrand Russell or Bergson or Maritain, but it was easy to see our warriors felt themselves well out of reach of Russell's scalpel. If no existential thought was ever considered in our Department of Philosophy, need we be astonished that none is expressed anywhere else among us?

You will surely have noticed by now that my chapter on the impasse in our thinking is almost as short as a dead-end street. I set out a plan; I say I will speak on the crisis in religion after I have spoken on the block in our thinking. I see right away that there is no practical way to disentangle thought and religion; they are hopelessly mixed, as they are among the Zulus. The profane is sacred; we bless our bridges and our restaurants, and by the same token the sacred is profaned because we mix it into everything. *Assueta vilescunt.* In joual, that means familiarity breeds contempt. That is why we must remain celibate and love only the polar star. If it rains two Sundays in succession,

*   Author of *Un homme et son Péché*, radio serial.
** Journalist with *Notre Temps*.

that is a punishment for feminine immodesty, but if it rains the day of pilgrimage, that is to try the faith of the just.

Take as an example the official manual, used in our normal schools, *The Philosophy and Theology of Education*. I will choose an important chapter, the one on Liberty. The problem is dismissed in three pages, three out of 194.

God respects our liberty. How could anyone imagine that the divine wisdom would not wish a free being to act freely? No power on earth can violate the free will of the human being. In the luminous wake of the Cross of Christ, martyrs have walked to their deaths, but their executioners could not rob them of their liberty to witness for the truth and to love God.

Because of the perfection of his nature man is free, but because of the very imperfection of that nature, his liberty is imperfect, and he is naturally liable to commit morally wrong actions. Sin exists. It is an undeniable fact. Beside those just men whose souls rest on the extended wings of the Cross of Christ, ready to take flight to Heaven, there is an army of sinners who are equally free to climb the cross in order to spit in the face of the Master. There lies the misery of human liberty. We consider that it is by the imperfection of liberty, not by its essence, that men are able to commit morally bad acts.

Even if you are not anti-clerical, you will agree that's not the strongest statement in the world. Yet we have found nothing better to feed the future teachers of our secondary schools, on a matter as important as the philosophy and theology of education. Here too the sacred and profane are confused. The volume is signed by a priest, Gérard Chaput, p.s.s. That makes it excellent.

Among priests also there is confusion. Because a man is a priest, he is prone to believe that everything he does is holy, including his little poetic itches. Nothing is more tiresome, dull, syrupy, disgusting, than the soft facility that oozes out works conceived under this delusion. Jean

Rostand takes more pains in lecturing on his frogs than Father Chaput on liberty.

We ought to know by this time that the confusion of the sacred and the profane regularly works to the detriment of the sacred. But we prefer to whine regularly over the excesses of the anti-clericals.

CHAPTER IV

QUEBEC'S JANSENIST
SHUDDERS

The Lord's Prayer, which is THE Prayer, doesn't ask to have things stay the same; it asks that things happen. It is not Prayer bogged down in the past, it is Prayer directed toward the future.

MYSELF

They say that people have had enough of religion. And the people who can't bear to hear talk about religion are the nice fat Catholics who are in fashion around here, you, you, you. Religious anxiety is not a plant that grows among us. Those who are deeply troubled by the religious question are not recruited among the ladies of Ste. Anne or the papal guards. Most French Canadians have had a bellyful of silliness and chatter on this subject. Still we have to talk about religion. There is no other serious problem. We began talking about joual and we notice that here we are describing the religious atmosphere of French Canada. That's the sign that we have but the one serious problem, that of spirituality.

However that may be, I have neither the intention nor the capacity to go into the matter exhaustively. I touched on it only indirectly in my letters to *Le Devoir;* it came about this way. The letter about speaking joual that I sent to Laurendeau and that he published started a chain re-

action. For four months there was a stream of letters to
Le Devoir about education, mostly from teachers, both
religious and lay. Laurendeau noticed that nobody wanted
his name printed, among all these who were protesting.
"Why all this fear?" he wondered.

The mail brings us letters all the time, mostly from
teachers and most of them interesting. But four times out
of five, our correspondent writes, 'Please don't publish my
name. My living depends on my anonymity.'

One man recalls to us the late Paul Hébert, 'ruined by
the authorities, because you published by mistake a private
letter written to one of your staff.' Another speaks of 'the
conspiracy of silence that surrounds our schools, as if the
expression of honest discontent would shake the Church.'
Every single one of them has his pseudonym all ready.
Apparently the teaching Brothers live in the same stifling
smog of fear. A characteristic ending says, 'Can I count
on your discretion? Please don't publish this letter. My
community is in enough trouble already. It gets nothing
except by long struggle; I would not want to cause any
more difficulties, and besides I would be the first to suffer.
I'm only glad to be of service to you.'

This paragraph closes a moderate and well-informed
letter, one that we would like to print because it expresses
clearly opinions based on experience. One of the joys of this
correspondence has been to find that there are cultured
men among the teaching Brothers, whose wits are still
alert in spite of the pressure on them, but who seem to
exist in complete solitude.

Where does such fear arise? Sometimes very material
considerations are mingled in it. One Brother writes, 'How
can one explain the outrageous monopolizing tactics of
some publishing houses? Real sharks, they are. We have
to crawl to them, we communities who are not in the good
graces of the above-mentioned publishers or of official
organizations, to get a few crumbs from their table in the
textbook section. *

---

* After 1940, when textbooks no longer came in from France,
certain religious communities were given assignments to write them.

We get some furious letters too; we suspect they may not be all they seem, though exasperation can sometimes bring out reactions of this kind. But now I am referring to reasonable letters, obviously written by thoughtful men. Why do those who write them so seldom feel that they can permit them to appear in public? Are they imagining things? Have they a persecution complex? It seems unlikely that so many good educators should all be victims of the same mania at the same time.

Then there must be some sort of persecution, some threat to freedom? And in the most important field of human activity, that in which our youth is trained? Whence comes this weight on human spirits, this trouble in breathing? Our correspondents are too discreet on that subject. We judge that they don't admit even to themselves what authority or group of authorities restricts their liberty.

This is unwholesome, this is serious. For if they don't know what goes on in the schools, who does? Perhaps the explanation of the many open failures which show up to surprise and scandalize us all lies here. If these men think it their duty to keep quiet, is the risk so great? What is its nature? What are they afraid of, and why?

The welcome mat was out. After long hesitation and with real pain, for I could foresee where my subject might lead me, I consulted a responsible priest and decided to send my answer to the question Laurendeau was asking. Here is the whole text of the reply, which appeared in *Le Devoir*, April 30, 1960.

Dear Mr. Laurendeau:

In your Friday column you asked, addressing teachers in general, 'What are you afraid of, and why?' Do you insist on your question? I mean, do you insist on an answer? Mr. J. C. Falardeau * will tell us again to examine our consciences. How many times a week are you frightened, my child? Of whom? Why? Never mind, here I go.

* Professor of Sociology at Laval.

The answer is simple enough. We are afraid of authority. Jean le Moyne said it in his famous article "The Religious Atmosphere of French Canada," written in 1951 and published in *Cité Libre,* of May, 1955. I wouldn't dream of trying to add to his masterly analysis; I take up the matter here only because I am sure that repetition is an important part of our education. We are afraid of authority; we live in a climate of magic, where under penalty of death we must infringe no taboo, where we must respect all the formulas, all the conformisms.

The pervading fear in which we live sterilizes all our efforts. If we write, all our propositions must be justifiable before possible inquisitors; if we act, all our actions must be measured by the traditional standard, that is, they must be repetitions of previous actions. We choose the safest way, to say nothing, to do nothing, to stand still. *Je me souviens!* (Quebec's motto.) Our doctors of theology, our doctors of philosophy, what do they do, what do they write? Their master, St. Thomas, wrote enough, fought enough, insulted enough people: *contra pestiferam doctrinam.* And he, Thomas Aquinas, said, that every excellent master leaves some writings behind him — *excellent master,* but not frightened copycat.

Nothing that is oppressive is Christian. Christianity is essentially a liberating force. One of these days French Canadians will discover that liberation. It is not Christianity that crushes us, but the triple spirit of evil. Of the three lusts which all men know, the one that scourges mankind most harshly is the third, the one of which nothing is said, the one never denounced from the pulpit, the spirit of domination. Do you know any preachers who denounce the snares of authority? Any professors who tell you to read St. Bernard's *Consideration?* Oh no, they always hammer on the same nail, as if our national vice was rebellion, as if we were not long since a dumb people, unable to express ourselves except by swearing and getting drunk.

They renounce money. They renounce sex. They never renounce power. Poor and chaste, but domineering, full of arrogance. 'The kings of the nations have lordship over them. But ye shall not be so, but he that is greater among you, let him become as the younger, and he that is chief as he that doth serve' (Luke XXIII, 25-27). This Christian revelation is the one least emphasized, this radical antithesis is skipped over. They make believe that Jesus Christ said nothing new about our relations with authority. Listen to Papini: "To command, to dominate, to appear the greatest, the richest, the handsomest, the wisest — all the history of mankind is nothing but terror of coming second" (*History of Christ*). Lanza del Vasto says: "The overthrow of authority is the first law of the Kingdom announced by the Messiah; for the two thousand years that he has predicted and preached this overthrow, Christianity has stubbornly pretended that nothing has been prescribed, nothing laid down on the subject" (*Commentary on the Gospel*).

They'll say, "But Papini and Lanza are not doctors of the Church." What about St. Peter? In the earliest days of the Church, at the moment when it was the time to assert authority, to show who was master, the centurion Cornelius appeared before Peter and knelt to him. Peter quickly raised him, saying, "Stand up. I too am a man" (*Acts*, X, 26). St. Augustine called his faithful disciples "Your holinesses," as we still address the Pope. We have come quite a way, but backward. In the time of St. Augustine a disciple stood up in full assembly to discuss something St. Augustine had said. Do you see any worker — or any learned man — nowadays who would get up in the cathedral to argue something with his bishop? Evidently that would mean that the man felt interested, deeply interested, in what his bishop said. It would mean too that there wasn't time for the constable to interfere. Finally it would mean that authority had a respect for man that we are not used to

True religion is not oppressive. It is magic, it is the witchdoctors that oppress us. If at times we feel oppressed by religion, then we are dealing with a caricature of religion. Pharisaism and Jansenism are all the same. Let me give you some examples from the environment I know well, part of our general situation. Our clergy is French Canadian, our teaching Brothers are French Canadian, our superiors are French Canadian. We are all cut from the same cloth. But it is not Jesus Christ, it is not even Rome, who forces on the nuns and to a lesser degree on the priests and brothers these absurd and anachronistic costumes; it is our Jansenism, our routine, our perfectionism, our timidity, our contempt for humanity. I do believe in the necessity of a distinctive dress for our priests and nuns. The function of such clothing is not solely to mask their sex — that would be soon done — but to signify their inner spirit. But I maintain that a costume need not be an irrational encumbrance in order to signify devotion to Jesus Christ. It can be rational, functional and symbolic all at once.

Nor is it Jesus Christ who imposes on us these slightly ridiculous names by which we intend to signify our separation from the world. We don't have to be called Brother Paphnace or Pancrase, Sister Sainte-Eulalie-du-Très-Saint-Sacrement or Sister Marie-du-Grand-Pouvoir in order to belong to Jesus Christ. I exaggerate? Read the report of the Council of Instruction's 1960 meeting—"...the Reverend Brothers Milon, Mélène, Martinien, Martony, Modestin...." Jesus was called Jesus, a significant name, fairly common among his people. He chose to dress like ordinary folk, so much so that Judas had to agree on a sign to identify him to the soldiers sent to arrest him in the Garden.

This kindly and protective authority, sometimes becoming harsh and vengeful, never consenting to talk things over with us, this is what we are afraid of. We are afraid of inspectors and commissioners. We risk losing our jobs (or of being sent back to the sticks to shut up). This tense and monolithic authority is convinced it cannot yield on a single point without risking the collapse of the whole edifice. It stands unapproachable until it hands down a condemnation; it never discusses anything.

I said a while ago that we are our own authorities; we engender each other, paternalism and slavery producing each other. He who has never known how to be free in an inferior position will never know how to lead when he has risen from the ranks. A people which has lost its taste for liberty corresponds to a touchy authority. The loss of the sense of liberty is widespread among us, not because of Catholic doctrine, but because of our petty and security-conscious way of living Catholicism.

When the Protestants left the paternal mansion (I might as well borrow John XXIII's metaphor) they carried some good with them, a small part of the heritage. We were left with the old property, the house and the equipment; they got away with a few pennies' worth of liberty. But they knew how to make what they had bear fruit. The object of ecumenism is to capitalize on all the Christian values together. No one argues that the Protestants have not known better than we how to preserve and develop some Christian values. Let's admit that they have better preserved the sense of liberty, which St. Thomas held to so strongly, but which since his day has been somewhat suspect for tactical though not dogmatic reasons.

Historically our Catholicism is a Catholicism of counter-Reformation. Add to that the conquest (Protestant) of Quebec, and you get our shrivelled, timid, ignorant Catholicism, reduced to a morality, a sexual morality at that, and even so, negative.

You will say I am wandering from my subject — no, I'm still on it. One small incident: one day I was looking around in the Laval University Press at Quebec. On the counter was a pile of *Cité Libre*. Two Brothers were sampling the forbidden fruit. They asked the salesman, "Is this any good, this review?" I broke in without being invited, "It's not only good, it's indispensable." One of them said to me, "A priest told us it was bad." To his mind, the case was judged; a priest had spoken.

Have you noticed, Mr. Laurendeau, that the only person who has answered your question, "What are they afraid of?" and who signed his name, was a retired lay teacher? Nobody can do anything to him, any more. Within the teaching Orders, I can see only Brother Clément Lockquell who seems to be reasonably free. I wonder how he did it and what he had to confront. He must have had a bravely protective Superior, one made of gold. I know that his book, *You the Chosen,* mild enough indeed, set some old teeth on edge. Anyhow he hasn't yet been excommunicated. The Christian Brothers have a long history, since they were founded 150 years ago. Being older than the rest of us, they are more free of restraint, more grown-up.

Here now is an extract from the Secondary School Program of Studies, 1958 edition. "In order to proceed in an orderly manner, those who hold positions are requested to communicate their observations to their directors or directresses, who will transmit them to their inspectors, and these to their chiefs." You see we have not yet got as far as God-the-Father who is in Quebec; we are only with the chiefs of the inspectors. What can be expected to remain after that filtering? No sound can pass through such a lot of stuffing, no light comes down through so many screens.

For those who have been slaves to try to be leaders is fatal. Those who have been under tyrants wait their chance to be tyrants themselves; those who are frightened wait their turn to frighten others. In the fable, the rabbit terrorizes the frogs. The teachers do not feel free, but I question if they try to free themselves. Where are the professors who not only tolerate discussion and questioning, but who provoke it? Where are the educators who are alive to the drama of our youth — the paralysis of communication — and who try to set free what struggles to break out? We shall never get anywhere if we educators do not make up our minds to liberate the captives, to do it systematically. It is so much simpler, more efficacious, more humane, more sensible even, than to wait for the slave revolt. Oppression is never perfectly watertight, personalities can never be entirely enclosed, but if they have been squeezed too long, souls find it hard not to hate. So we recover only the newly free, like the newly rich. What do we read every Saturday in *Le Devoir*? The half-quarrelsome, half-bitter confessions of those who were forbidden to read Mauriac and who read him all the same. They boast of it now, like the bold boys who whistle when the good Brothers pass by on their way to vespers. We must avoid such losses; we cannot afford to lose any talents, any brains. Instead of restricting liberty we should under-take to make it part of our education — offer Montherlant to the lad who has his eye on Mauriac, travel two miles with the man who asks us to go a mile, according to the teaching of the Sermon on the Mount.

I am still sort of unhappy, for I haven't said clearly what we are afraid of. We are afraid of authority because we haven't the courage of liberty. In place of whining, let us confess that we love the word liberty, but what we really want is security. To want both and to grumble over having security without liberty is what everybody does. Teachers ought to do better than that — that unfocused fear and unadmitted cowardice. It isn't brilliant, it isn't even French Canadian, it's just good old human nature from way back. The other evening I was talking with a bus driver — we happened to be alone. He complained of inspectors and stoolies, of abusive demoralizing controls. Who then is free? Only the man who has nothing to lose, Socrates, Jesus, Gandhi, John XXIII. (He has a sense of humour, a good sign.)

Only three weeks after this letter came out, May 21st, 1960, Mr. Amédée Francoeur sent the following in reply. I include it here because I find it typical of the devout Quebec mentality. As you will see, Mr. Francoeur has understood nothing, and besides he questions my motives. A man I know wrote me, "The Francoeurs are little boys. Someone has pasted together a few prejudices for them, to take the place of philosophy and religion until the day they die. Their only reaction is to defend their stand, their only defence is to question the motives of others."

Here is Mr. Francoeur's letter :

Dear Brother Untel,

When I read your article on fear, I was at once filled with compassion for you and your colleagues. Poor little martyrs, under pressure and tyranny from your arbitrary and domineering superiors. Between the lines, I think I can see the germ of anarchy growing in your heart. If you ever succeed in your little revolution, you will, like all anarchists, rush to grab the power you seem to desire so ardently. I sincerely pity your subordinates, who will have, as you say, a slave risen from the ranks to rule over them, a slave who, oppressed and frightened, will strive to oppress and frighten in turn. In fact, aren't you one of those who have had a little power and lost it, and so turn their rancour against anything that has to do with authority? Why the devil use St. Thomas as a screen to make us believe in this phony oppression of which you are victim, and to set yourself up as a hero who will redeem the captives? That smacks of your own conceit.

You appear to have studied a little philosophy, but I think you would do better to have a philosophy of life that sees the good side of things. Someone says, "A little science leads away from God, a great deal leads back to him." Do some more studying.

Poor martyr, you suffocate. Before letting yourself be stifled by those proud and domineering superiors, free yourself, you who seem to cherish liberty so much. Pass through the iron curtain around you and breathe the fresh air of a free and democratic city. Or make a retreat under the wise and enlightened guidance of a holy director of conscience. Apparently you don't know that true liberty consists in continuing to accept voluntarily what you deliberately accepted once, and even what is imposed on you. Your comparison between St. Augustine questioned by a hearer and a Christian doing the same thing with his bishop in the cathedral seems forced to me. St. Augustine had to answer many questions posed by his disciples, by pagans, by cynical heretics, and often this happened in public places. Console yourself, in the United States this sort of thing is done by Catholic priests who raise questions and answer them on street corners, like the Salvation Army.

With regard to costume, aren't you a little bold to compare yourself to Jesus? He chose deliberately to become one of the common people and consequently to wear their dress. In his time there were no teaching Brothers, but priests wore a special costume, with phylacteries. Don't forget that Jesus, in spite of the tyranny of his religious superiors, told the people, 'Do what they tell you to do.'

Isn't it pretty strong for a Brother to present Protestants as heroes of liberty? It is true that you have, as you say, a shrivelled and timid Catholicism. That excuses you. Their free thought is precisely one of the major weak points in their doctrine.

I must end this diatribe. I believe it will encourage you to bear higher the standard of the timid and of those who live underground in silence.

Amédée Francoeur.

P.S. You will tell me I am an extremist. Aren't you too? At least we can sympathize on that point.

· · ·

Some colleagues of mine, speaking for men of our profession and signing themselves "A group of professors," amused themselves by replying.

To Brother Amédée,

If Brother Untel had had you as a novice master and you had given him a few scoldings as you know how to do, he would not be today the rebellious gamin that you enjoyed slapping down in *Le Devoir*. Between you and me, Amédée, instead of reading between the lines, you ought just to have gathered some plain thoughts from the lines. You would not have made a gay fellow who likes camembert and brandy into a virgin martyr. It is false that Brother Anonymous lusts for power, it is false that Brother Anonymous has ever had the least bit of power. He has never had anything but influence. Since when, my dear Amédée, has a philosophy of life consisted in looking on the bright side? We thought it consisted in seeing things as they are, good and evil. 'Free yourself'? Cowardly advice, advice of a weakling. When you feel able to liberate the slaves, you stay with them. That was the wise advice of an unbeliever, Alain: 'The day when well-balanced and learned men shall be slaves and live among them, there will be no more slaves.'

Your definition of true liberty is not French. We doubt if it is even Thomist. We are sure that Brother Anonymous, who has 'done a little philosophy,' really knows nothing of your definition. The only liberty he claims is the liberty to talk things over with his superiors, an essentially Christian liberty. A worthy attitude before a superior is precisely what ought to distinguish our society. That is why Brother Anonymous calls our attention to the scene of Peter and the centurion. The core of his article is 'Stand up, I also am a man.' You didn't take that in because you were so busy reading between the lines.

Not the friar (inferior) but the French Canadian speaks from the mouth of Brother Anonymous. You make him out a neurotic, an anarchist, who wants to throw off his cassock. 'True liberty,' my friend, 'permits observations and suggestions. They are not a sign of rebellion, but form the substance of intelligent obedience' (Mgr. Roberts, S.J.). To put oneself voluntarily and freely into the hands of others is not to vow to see with their eyes and speak with their lips."

I myself (Frère Untel) could not abandon the field of battle. I returned to the charge with a very different piece of work, more serene but not at all repentant. I shall call this article, without too much reason, "Journal of a Timid Man." *Le Devoir*, June 14, 1960.

"Of What are They Afraid?" has just appeared in *Le Devoir*. I await the reactions. Someone close to me has already judged it: it is not even Catholic.

I have been talking with a priest. He tells me that the patron saint of French Canadians ought to be *Notre Dame de la Trouille*. I must explain to the younger generation that *trouille* is a slang word meaning extreme, permanent fear, an institutional fear. To the devout I must explain that this title is no more irreverent than that of the edifying film in which François Rozet played, *Notre Dame de la Mouise, mouise* being a slang term for black misery, absolute destitution. We ought to raise a basilica to *Notre Dame de la Trouille* and organize some pilgrimages.

I have received some letters from my colleagues telling me of their enthusiasm on reading my article. One of them tells me, "You are a kind of symbol of our right to live. I wish you luck, even if the day comes when you will be nothing but a silent symbol for us." I had a phone call from the Brothers of another community than mine, assuring me of their support. There are those who agree with me and those who disagree — one can't displease everybody.

Think what you like. I don't report these things out of vanity or complacency — I am no Narcissus. I don't say that I take no pleasure in them; I do take pleasure, and almost happiness, but I report them to prove that I have been right to denounce our common fear. I am not then a paranoiac. Our fear is real, more real than I can say.

One letter says, "Your article gives an impression of good nature which makes even stronger the feeling of great and living tension expressed between the lines." The man who wrote that, a layman, is my friend. He has felt truly that I allow myself some digressions, some bits of nonsense, on purpose. I have to write in a relaxed, unconstipated kind of way. I must struggle against fear formalism, conformity; even in my style I must reject timidity. Rabelais cried from the towers of Notre Dame to the pale, super-intellectual men of the Renaissance, "There is also the body." From the depths of our fear and our conformism, we must cry out and show even in our style that we have had enough of Quebec's Jansenist shudders.

I dismiss in advance the free-thinking anti-clericals who are going to rub their hands when they read these avowals from a Brother, and the frightened devotees, who will cry dirty-bird. The former did not wait for my writings to do their sniggering. To the others I say that it is better to be caught cleaning out the nest, which I am doing in my own way, than shamefully hiding the manure. (What language, my dear Brother, what language! Go wash out your mouth!)

Abbé Dion and Abbé O'Neill are the seed of the Church for the future harvest. The Province of Quebec is on the move. We are among the few western nations who have known neither political revolution nor major religious crisis. We shall have no revolution; the proximity of our Anglo-Saxon neighbours guarantees that. They would not let us do any damage. Perhaps even the Twenty-second Regiment (the Vandoos), commanded in English, would put it down. No revolution at all. But what we are going to see take place is the disaffection of the French Canadian people from their religion. Things are already more spoiled than shows on the surface. The pilgrimages to Notre Dame du Cap and Ste. Anne de Beaupré ought not to fool us. In Spain too (Spanish Catholicism, does that mean anything to you, Mr. Jean Le Moyne?) * the places of pilgrimage were very popular right up to 1936. The priests were held in high honour. Until the day they were shot, more than a thousand of them in the diocese of Barcelona alone.

Spoiled beyond what we can see — the young people whom we teach in class are as far from Christianity as they

* Jean Le Moyne as editor of *La Nouvelle Relève*, supported the Spanish Republic.

can go without making a commotion. Their ideas, their feelings, above all their feelings about money, women, success, love are as foreign to Christianity as is possible. The failure of our religious teaching is plain. Yet what French Canadian has not lived for years under the influence of a cassock, or at least under the rule of one?

Would religion in our society survive the disappearance of the religious apparatus? In other words, are we as individuals standing upright on the basis of religion, or are we held up by the ears? In my first letter, I asked (Brother Anonymous cites Brother Anonymous) if we should work for a major crisis which would wake us up, but at a price. It seems that we shall not avoid a general disaffection from religion — we already have that. There will be no other crisis, no other outcry. Everything will happen calmly, politely, painlessly, the way a cathedral is swallowed up in an abyss.

There can be no continuity. Providentially, a few men have already set up their tents on the other side, the side of the future. Abbé Dion and Abbé O'Neill are not the only ones, but they have the value of symbols and that's why they are the only ones I name. About them and those like them religion will be reorganized in the French Canadian world of tomorrow. In the free city of tomorrow there will still be priests. Mr. Jean-Charles Falardeau seems a little shocked at that (*Cité Libre,* June-July 1960).

As to the failure of our religious instruction, the sad hearts comfort themselves so long as the official programs and examinations go on. They tell themselves that what is essential is assured. So many thousand hours of religious instruction in the Province each year. The hearts of the administration are overflowing with satisfaction.

But what does this religious instruction produce? Abbé Yvon Roy, who is not an extremist (there are no extremists in the Seminary of Quebec) reported in his memoire to the Laval Faculty of Arts that "out of three thousand students whom we now have at the University, are there

ten to whom the existence of God is evident?" He
wondered, the Abbé Roy, and the pupils he was wonder-
ing about were those coming from the classical colleges.
The pupils who come from the public courses are certainly
no better off. Who was it was saying that in Montreal only
two institutions give a religious training which is not a
deformation, the *Collège Marie-de-France* and the *Collège
Stanislas?**

My dear little Brother Anonymous, my little blue
rabbit, are you going to tell me why you write such things,
smack in the face of the Province?

I write such things out of charity. Please don't laugh,
why shouldn't I have a spark of charity? One person loves
music and he says so and nobody laughs; another loves the
work of Camus and he says so and nobody laughs. It is
quite possible that I love French Canadians a little bit and
want to talk to them. I live at the end of the world and I
long to talk with a few men.

I write also to prove that I can say what I think, to prove
that all truth is good to say. My own idea is that we are
freer than we think, that it isn't liberty that is lacking,
but the courage to use the liberty that we have. We whine
about lost liberty, and don't try what we have. Like the
dog in the Jules Renard story we feel the chain that no
longer binds us. Speaking as a Canadian, I say shall we
take the plunge and be free?

At this time of year, our institutions exchange monitors
for the exams. I betake myself to the Convent, and a nun
comes to watch my class. She is a teaching Sister, not a
cloistered nun, but she tells me that she is not authorized
to come alone to our college. She must be accompanied by
another Sister or a pupil. The College is only two blocks
from the Convent, and this is broad daylight in the middle
of 1960. That's what we have made of the liberty of Jesus
Christ. That's what I am thinking of when I say I write
out of charity. Man is despised in the Province of Quebec.

* Both originally French foundations.

"Take care that asceticism or the ascetic way of life in your communities does not become a barrier or a cause of failure. We speak of certain customs which, if they had meaning in some other cultural context, have none today, and because of which some truly good and brave young girl may find herself hindered in her religious vocation." Who said that? Pius XII to the General Superiors of the Women's Communities.

Why do the writings of the two Abbés, their principal books, cause so much commotion? Read and reread these texts, and you will find nothing to justify the hysteria of the beadles. Far from being extravagant, their works are perfectly moderate, prudent and calm. Indeed they are far more calm, more polite, than the texts of the virtuous inquisitors who denounce them. For *The Christian and the Elections*, by Abbé Dion and Abbé O'Neill, is not even a precision instrument, a subtle, delicate mechanism; it is not even esoteric theology. Rather it is elementary, a bit coarse, not a fine saw but a bludgeon — and they both wield it. It's homemade bread, not French pastry. And because it is neither bitter nor anarchistic, it has brought forth yells. The Powers-that-be must have tender hides to squall like scalded cats over these books. They must be scared — that's it, they are terribly afraid, our Powers. All their claws are out at the first little noise. In the land of Quebec, everything can be explained by fear, from the bewilderment of the little people to the fidgets of the great.

A few years ago Filion called for a Bernanos. We don't need a Bernanos; he is much too strong for us, we could never pick ourselves up after him. No, what we need is a humorist, somebody like Chesterton or Jerome K. Jerome. I wish we had a bishop who would call himself Jerome K. Jerome, and who would air out the Province by making gentle fun of our taboos, our terrors, our conformities, simply by saying "Two plus two equals four." A kind of John XXIII on the Quebec scale would shake up our routines.

A part of the élite among us has no roots. They are cultivated, refined, anything you like, but far away from us, exiles within their own country. The teaching Brothers, on the other hand, are well rooted in their environment. We're the real thing, crows hatched in our woods, saplings well provided with roots. Now we ought to put out branches, show what we can do in our own trade, which is to educate in all fields. Christians are the salt of the earth, the Brothers are the salt of education.

According to the contented slaves, authority all over the world is a poor little thing, in danger. It is a fragile plant that cannot be too carefully protected. It lives under a glass jar — don't touch. The contrary is true. Authority has never been so crushing, so omnipresent, so efficient. It has reached the point where hardly a free man is left in the world. We needn't go back to the Deluge to establish that fact, it is enough to consider how things are at the moment. Half of mankind is under the yoke of Communism, a little authority that is not too fragile. We can't say these days that it is weak and battered in the fight.

Neither can we say that authority is weak in our own countries. Our authorities break us in and then they do as they please. Anyhow we are easy to rule. In fact it is paper that governs us, mere sets of forms. Just see with what touching good will, with what conscientiousness, we fill out forms; we spend dozens of hours making little marks in little squares. Any green official from the Department can floor a roomful of teachers, merely by giving them forms to fill out. To enjoy defending the authorities in 1960, you have to be a contented cuckold type.

And religious authority, my little Brother Anonymous, do you put that with the others?

Authority used in Christian fashion is not crushing. The yoke of Jesus Christ is light — no pun, but gospel truth. (The pun is on the name of Cardinal Léger, Archbishop of Montreal — *léger,* light.) John XXIII doesn't crush anybody. My Superiors in the community — I know them well

— are not tyrannical. That's why I maintain that on the whole the Brothers are less frightened, noticeably freer, than the ordinary run of French Canadians.

But then, my little Brother, you contradict yourself. The other day you were proclaiming your fear of authority, and now you say your Superiors are kindly fathers. I don't understand.

It's not an exaggeration. The Brothers are made of the same clay as other French Canadians; we have our share of fraidycats. I must say at once that I am speaking only of my own experience. Intelligent people will understand that there is some motive in my affectation of fear. When a man is really scared, he keeps quiet, or he flatters his enemy. If I speak out, it is not because I am so brave, but because I have nothing to lose.

I am a foot-soldier, I have never held power. And anyone will grant that I'm not taking the usual means to grasp it. That's why, in my own surroundings, I feel free, as a hungry wolf feels free. If I speak it is to say to others: it's up to you, my fine fellow, to be as thin as I am.

I can say now, let him who will believe me, that I am neither unhappy nor tied up in knots nor rebellious. When a man speaks for himself to other men, directly, with no other guarantee than a certain tone of voice, he is believed or rejected on his own word. I am not unhappy; neither do I play about like a baby whale all day long. I am as I am, neither happy nor unhappy. But I have no desire to leave the Order, to *demoiner,* which in our community slang means to return to secular life. I say this without boasting, but with a certain humility. By the grace of God and the tolerance of the Virgin Mary (and of my Superiors) I intend to die a Brother, Brother Anonymous unto eternity. If I argue, it is simply because I want to stay here, at home with the Brothers. I and those like me will live in the house of the future.

"My old comrades, old brothers, we shall arrive one day at the gates of the Kingdom of God. A worn and harassed band, white with the dust of the roads, with beloved harsh faces where the sweat has dried, with eyes that have looked on good and evil, fulfilled their task, accepted life and death, and never surrendered" (Bernanos).

Those final words above all, how they appeal to me! Eyes that have never surrendered, neither rebellious nor whining, neither complacent nor cringing, simply an eye that does not surrender. One can demand that much of oneself, to be an eye that does not surrender.

* * *

You remember that in my "Journal of a Timid Man", I called for a response from the Sisters. It was long in coming. Nevertheless, I was almost sure that I had made no mistake in speaking of the Sisters as I had done in my two previous articles. I received a few echoes from individuals that confirmed my suspicions, but I needed a reply that would be accepted by everyone as authentic. It burst out in *Le Devoir* July 18, 1960. For better or worse, I think I am not wrong in calling Sister Anonymous' (Soeur Une Telle's) letter historic.

SISTER ANONYMOUS
TO BROTHER ANONYMOUS

For a long time I have wanted to congratulate you on the courageous attitude you show in this matter of the education of the young children and of the older boys and girls. Today I have a moment after the completion of the revisions, the compilations, corrections, annotations, and of the graduation exercises. I am awaiting the holy annual retreat — you know that a teaching Sister's life duplicates that of a teaching Brother. At last I can hold out to you a fraternal and sympathetic hand, offering you my humble approbation.

Brother Anonymous, you say out loud what all of us teaching Sisters think to ourselves. Yes, as you say, we are turned in upon ourselves, we are afraid, we have this ingrained fear. Shall I confide to you that our Mothers Superior (I'm using a euphemism here) are more suspicious than your Brothers Superior? So if she were ever identified, the writer of this letter would be first beheaded and then destroyed.

And you, Brothers, don't your Superiors ever scold you? Once in a while, do they condescend to realize that the odd specimens are more precious than the others?

Brother Anonymous, you speak the very truth when you mention that in order to exchange examination monitors the nun who leaves the convent must be accompanied by another Sister, who in turn must be accompanied lest she have to make the return journey alone, from one corner of the street to the other. That's how it is with us. Just lately I came upon an even crazier situation. A Sister had to look for someone to go with her to answer the telephone in another wing of her big convent. To be sure, this was a cloistered order. But what do you think of our having to be accompanied when we go to confession at the church next door? Rather an embarrassing rite, not to say deadly.

I know some of my fellow nuns who had to give up courses of study they had begun brilliantly because there was no other nun in the same convent taking courses in the same faculty. These everlasting and indiscriminating accompanyings get on your nerves and produce more distrust. Are the active communities that are free from all this surveillance more wicked than we? The Little Sister of the Poor who goes alone and cheerfully down any street, has she ever been kidnapped?

Are laymen any more edified by the sight of two nuns cackling and whispering together than by the behaviour of one alone, dignified and minding her own business? What would our Pope John think of all this, he who knew so well how to break with outworn customs?

The alarming lack of recruits in a great teaching community which every year graduates hundreds and hundreds of young girls is due to this lack of fresh air, this failure to adapt to the social needs of our time. Our youth today takes on its responsibilities early, though I grant you it talks joual. It can tell from a long way off whether a place is run efficiently or not. It wants what it wants, and it turns up its nose at these pious affectations which put such a curb on personality.

'Pure, proud, conquering, joyous,' is the slogan of Catholic Action. A good many girls have defended and practised it during their student years. Some have even won converts among the Guides and the school and parish organizations, the sport clubs and the like. Then how must appear to them the state of contention, of paralysis they detect among their teachers, when they themselves are impatient of pettiness, of hesitation and delays? In spite of our undeniable success in keeping ourselves pure — and we are thoroughly so — how can we attain to pride and joy and victory when our hands are tied, our hearts full of impossible dreams, our eyes fixed on the dead lamps of formalism? 'The letter killeth, the spirit giveth life' (II Cor. III, 3).

Brother, I love the Sisters, the best people in the world. I love myself, but how I would like to have them more accessible, more open to human feelings, more outgiving, more *women!* It is a lot to say. It seems to me our Spouse would love us the more for it.

They fill the ears of us Sisters — of course I know the Brothers less—with exhortations to be mature, to be adult. But how can anyone become adult, good Lord, with such a mess of childish nonsense imposed on us under the head of 'spiritual infancy?' If any brave subject sticks its head out of this heap of banal, oldfashioned, bygone material, the poor thing is soon buried deeper than ever, bruised by our so-called maternal hands. Fright invades the flock. It it best to keep quiet and wait. Wait for what? I wouldn't know.

Brother Anonymous, I am not learned, I can't quote St. Thomas Aquinas and Bossuet and Plato from memory; I only try to use what sense the good Lord gave me. Television is another of our problems. It appears that this is an invention of the devil, which would bring about the ruin of the religious spirit in our convents. Nevertheless, Brother, how many television antennae I descry on the most respectable roofs — bishoprics, colleges, hospitals, universities, presbyteries. In all the convents of our Order such an apparatus is strictly forbidden. Our older pupils, who live at home, bring in every day like a charitable gift the bits of literary, scientific, and political information they have picked up at home, watching the screen between papa and mama. Our contemporary masters indeed present magnificent educational programs. The teaching Sister can see nothing, hear nothing of them. Our duty to be ahead of the times is not equal to the task. Ought we not to explore for our own benefit these audio-visual methods, ought we not to be able to talk about them in class, at recreation? How guide our pupils when our ears are hermetically closed? What do you think?

I end here (soon to return) a letter which I have tried to make thoughtful and exact. I am violent by nature, but thoughtful by training. These considerations of mine have lightened my subconscious a little — a subconscious that threatened to explode in my solitude. You can see, Brother Anonymous, that I am not malicious. My arguments are rather gentle. I am used to wearing a muzzle; when I take to my pen, prudence requires anonymity. Goodbye!

This letter stupefied the good Sisters. From all corners of the Province, Chicoutimi, Ottawa (sic), Montreal, Quebec, Nicolet, Ste-Anne-de-la-Pocatière, echoes reached me by way of my colleagues who were taking their summer courses. The consensus was that Sister Anonymous was ill, mad, or a maladjusted nun who was working off her spitefulness, if in truth she was a nun. She was suspected of being Brother Anonymous or some sacrilegious pretender to the nun's headdress. Some explanation for such outbreaks is always ready, in someone's pocket or handbag. Brother Anonymous is a layman in disguise, Sister Anonymous is a man, and so on.

I see only two alternatives to these cringing judgments and absurd hypotheses: either the Sister's statements are false and scandalous, or they are not. The examples of pharisaical meanness and irrational practices which she gives could be multiplied a hundred times. We have them all hot to set before the innocent. Canon Jacques Leclercq attacks them even more sharply than Sister Anonymous, with the *imprimatur** to boot, in his book *The Religious Vocation*. Speaking of the anachronisms that weigh down certain forms of the religious life, especially in the women's communities, he writes:

All this provokes a reaction against forms which have become unintelligible or have only folklore value. When a young girl who has gone out alone since she was a child enters a convent where she may not go out unaccompanied, she feels this is hateful and absurd. The rule was established at a time when an honourable woman of a certain rank never went out alone; if she had she would have risked being disagreeably accosted. The nuns of the Orders in question were considered as belonging to good society. The young girls of our day cannot take such rules seriously. If the religious life is sown with such usages, it will be the religious life itself as seen in the Orders which she will not be able to take seriously.

Again, it is traditional in most Orders for the nuns to kneel when they address their Superior. In other times this was a normal usage, resembling forms of respect employed in life outside the convents, but it has no basis for existing in the present day. When a girl enters a convent where this kind of thing goes on, she gets the impression of having gone back three hundred years, instead of being initiated into a world of supernatural reality.

Pius XII sounded the same note:

You wish to serve the cause of Jesus Christ and His Church according to the needs of the present. Then it is not reasonable to persist in customs and manners that hinder such service or perhaps make it impossible. The teaching Sisters and the women educators ought to be well prepared and equal to their tasks. They must be familiar with what-

---

* Imprimatur is the official (ecclesiastical) licence to print.

ever youth has to come in contact with and whatever it is likely to be influenced by, so that pupils will not hesitate to tell each other, 'We can go to Sister with our problems and our difficulties; she will understand and help.'

You are right, Sister Anonymous, Pius XII asks you to keep in touch with everything that affects youth — but you have to depend on your students to keep you in touch with what goes on outside your walls. Not only can you not solve their problems, but you create some that will remain forever insoluble for those who enter your ranks.

The statements of Sister Anonymous are indeed scandalous, in the dictionary sense of the word scandal — something that makes us stumble, something that calls for a straightening up. A straightening up that may be a trifle nerve-racking, accompanied by some palpitations, but in the long run a straightening up. The reaction of the Sisters, as a body and so far as we know, was very different from that of the Brothers to Brother Anonymous. The Brothers, like good sports, approved, while the Sisters almost unanimously rejected Sister Anonymous. They withdrew from her as one, a very feminine reaction. "Woman," said Alain, "is the refusal to accept the fact." Like everything human, this refusal of the fact is ambiguous. Among the lowly, it is caprice and stupidity, that feminine stupidity which is the greatest affliction among all the stupidities under the sun. Among the greater souls, this refusal of the fact becomes a source of resilience, of renewal, of freshness. With St. Mary, it is the foundation of our hoping against hope. We say to ourselves, St. Mary will set things right, she will not resign herself to this state of affairs, with patience she will find the way to save us; she will find the weak point in the adversary's armour, as the root finds the crack in the rock.

The Sisters then, refuse to recognize the facts that stare them in the face. They deny Sister Anonymous, they try to shut her off in neurosis. Feminine conformity and solidarity play their part. Taken singly, the Sisters will readily admit the truthfulness of Sister Anonymous' observations. We know a good many of them personally and we have their testimony.

PART II

Brother Anonymous
Softens Up

In this second part of my book, after getting rid of my bile in the former chapters, I'm going to be sweeter than honey. I can't be rough all the time. First, I want to talk to the lay teachers about the demand for quality in their work and about how urgent it is that the women teachers grow up politically. These are matters I think they ought to discuss in considering the building up of their professional associations.

Then, in my second chapter, I shall be writing to the new members of the teaching communities. Nothing is so like one teaching brotherhood as another teaching brotherhood. The seven or eight of them in Quebec differ from each other about as much as two marks of brandy — or if you're a prohibitionist, as two bottles of coke. The "Letter to a Young Brother," though addressed to a limited class of citizens, still has some general interest. Everything that is human always concerns all men. "The road from man to man goes round the world."

CHAPTER I

THIS MATRIARCHAL
SYSTEM

I could not hope to be of use to you, the lay teachers, if I did not bear in mind that we always have to receive our souls from the hands of others. It is the others who give us to ourselves, who define us, in the etymological sense of the word, set boundaries for us, put us in our places, hem us in. I want to give you into your own hands, that is to your own minds. It was written, "In the beginning God created man and gave him over to his own counsel" (Ecclesiasticus XV, 14). So I address myself to your intelligence. I have no taste for playing pretty tunes, for appealing to your prejudices (we all have them), or to your superficial feelings and sentimentality. The language of reason is austere, but it leads to liberty, which is never outside the limits of our knowledge. The quality of our knowledge measures the degree of our liberty. To sum up, I rely on your love of truth.

I want to recall part of the theme of Education Week: Teachers ought to form a team. I mean here by teachers all who are engaged in education, rank and file as well as superiors. This leads me to define rapidly the teaching profession and to say a word about the links that ought to exist among teachers, horizontally and vertically.

It is harder than appears at first sight to say exactly what we mean by profession, professional, trade. The dictionaries are not much help; trade and profession are not contrasted with each other. We must turn to current usage, which though not the final court of appeal, is the only real criterion, the master of true language, according to St. Thomas. French Canadian usage reserves the terms profession and professional for certain activities and refuses them to others. To be sure we're talking about the same thing, let's take a few examples. Here in Quebec no one dreams of saying that a plumber, a mason, a lumberjack, a carpenter, a salesman, a grocer or a farmer is a professional. These men may be labourers, civil servants, artisans; they are not professionals.

On the other hand, everyone agrees that an engineer, a lawyer, a doctor, a notary, is a professional. Pick out two of these examples, a plumber and a lawyer. The one is a man with a trade, the other has a profession. What is the intrinsic difference between these two terms? I think there are four factors that distinguish trades and professions: the difference in the preparation required, the difference in the intellectual effort involved in the practice of one or the other, the difference in the material with which they work, and the difference in the structures of the organizations to which they belong. Let me explain a little.

Usually a trade requires little academic preparation. Four years at most is enough to learn it, and those four years come at the end of the ninth year of schooling. Then a boy can be ready, other things being equal, to practise his trade at eighteen or twenty, even where the requirements are the most stringent. A profession requires twenty years of schooling, with five or six years of that at the University, so that a professional does not begin to exercise his profession before he is twenty-seven or eight. The difference is enormous, especially taking into account the particular importance of these early years.

The man with a trade needs to make a physical effort.

or at all events to have a certain manual skill, while the professional works mainly with his head, as people say.

And the third difference is the most important of all. A trade is concerned with the manufacture or upkeep of material things, while a profession is dedicated to the service of mankind. There need be no difficulty in classifying the engineer; he is principally a handler of men, even when he is building a dam, throwing a bridge across a river, or driving through a superhighway. He is more occupied with men than with matter. Let me sum up my ideas in a formula: trades deal with matter, professions deal with men.

Now let us see if teachers are professionals, or men with a trade, or merely civil servants. On the last point, the service of mankind, clearly the teacher is a professional; he deals with men and not with matter. On the second point, the preponderance of the exercise of the intellect over that of muscle, our work is set squarely among liberal activities, the activities we call professional.

You foresee where I am going to hesitate — at the first point, the academic requirements. I think the preparation that most of us have cannot class us as professionals. Face the facts. It's no use to cross the street to dodge the doctor when you're ill, it's no use to refuse an X-ray for fear of the sanitarium, and it is not only vain but primitive to work up a bad temper when our wounds are exposed. The only civilized, healthy, progressive attitude is to accept the facts.

How do things stand? Young men and women finish their eleventh year, take two years at normal school and emerge consecrated professionals? They are twenty or perhaps twenty-two. The real professional begins his career when he is nearly thirty. At best, supposing that our eleventh year student goes on to his A certificate, that makes only fifteen years in school, the equivalent of the B.A. degree. But the professional adds five or six years at the University to his B.A. If we don't measure up to professional status, the gap is here. Then shall we say that we are abbreviated professionals, and that our profession is a bargain-basement product?

If we take a good look at our situation, we shall see that we must bend all our efforts to better our preparation if we are to deserve the title and prestige attached to the liberal professions. The improvement of academic quality among us must be our constant care, for it is the key to all our problems. We shall be respected, we shall be decently paid, we shall be given consideration when we are qualified to be. Quality does not necessarily go along with big salaries; the big salaries will follow quality.

The contribution we make in our school work also depends on the excellence of our general academic preparation. The most valuable teaching abilities are rooted in the excellence of our knowledge and not in the mastery of the little tricks of the trade. The outstanding professor of mathematics or French is first of all the one who knows his math and his French thoroughly, not the one who has a few tricks up his sleeve.

The final difference between a profession and a trade is the kind of organization they provide themselves with. Men in trades are grouped in unions, professionals in various kinds of associations. Doctors have their College, lawyers their Bar, notaries their Chamber, engineers their Corporation. There is some diversity in this terminology. Only the College of Physicians and Surgeons and the Bar rest on a long tradition of exclusiveness in name and fact. The functions of these diverse associations, what I would call their bases, are almost diametrically opposed. The union works to protect its members, at least up to the present time. The professional groups work to protect the public. Union activity is directed toward improving conditions of work and pay of members; the professional group operates to improve the quality of the service it offers the public. Another thing, the union is governed by labour laws imposed from without, while the professionals govern themselves, police themselves (if I may say so) and set their own standards.

Here I would like to emphasize an idea put forward by Mgr. Lussier, Rector of the University of Montreal, in a lecture given before the Federation of Catholic Teachers of Quebec in November, 1957. He told them, in substance, that they will truly raise themselves to the professional level, will rise above the trade-union status, on the day when the grievance committee becomes less important than the committee on professional advancement. The genuinely professional arguments and claims among professional men ought to be settled among themselves. Doctors determine the standards and requirements of the medical profession; teachers must determine their standards and requirements. Until we do that, we shall not be professionals. We labour in vain pretending to be; we are not.

If we give up trying, it is we who contemn ourselves, not our bosses or the public. No one denies us quality; we deny it to ourselves, through laziness, conventionality, contempt of ourselves.

Now that I have defined what a profession is, I want to say a word on the relationships which ought to exist among professionals when those professionals happen to be teachers. As to the relationships which I call horizontal, I refer you to M. de la Palice*. He will tell you that to form a team you have to meet together first. Let me make a concrete suggestion. Why not hold meetings of the entire staff every week, in schools where this is not done already? I say entire staff, religious and lay, masculine and feminine. We are all engaged in the same exacting adventure. I am ashamed to admit that we have

* This means that the proposition is self-evident.

only had such meetings at the school where I work since the beginning of the year, and now we find them such a help that we wonder how we got along without them for so long. The procedure is simple enough. We meet every Thursday after classes. The first part is a little like church on Sunday, with remarks by the principal, announcements, all that kind of thing. Then the teachers ask questions on this and that, request information, and call for clarification of some matters; answers are given informally in the spirit of comradeship which the common practice of a difficult trade engenders. Finally, as the main part of the meeting, one of the teachers gives a talk on some point in the program, science, French, or whatnot. It is well to keep minutes of these meetings, to ensure their efficiency and smooth working. Such records are useful to recall later what was decided on — many a decision, many a project has never amounted to anything for the simple reason that nobody remembered it.

These meetings have the great advantage of spreading around information, and also, I'd say, uneasiness. It is important for all the members of a teaching staff to know about a problem at the same time, to discuss possible solutions, in a word, to vibrate on the same pitch. Problems don't grow less of themselves, we should have no illusions about that. We are only beginning to realize their depth and complexity. We have to close ranks. *Noblesse oblige, profession oblige.*

I read this small item the other day in a newspaper: a Catholic Archbishop, Mgr. John Heenan of Liverpool, told his faithful that if they had to choose between going to a union meeting and going to a religious service, they should choose the union meeting. There you can see the importance the Church attaches to the work these organizations do. The Church knows very well that the sacrifice required of men in our day is not so much to cut down on their eating as to cut down on their leisure time. That's why the Church has relaxed the rules on fasting. Let the doctors look after the eating. What is required of men nowadays is to devote more time to the common good.

The world we shall continue to live in will be more and more complex. More and more we shall have to get together to talk over our problems, more and more the best and most enlightened among us will have to help the rest. Some men ought to give two, three and four evenings a week to this common good, perhaps to take part in a discussion on education, or to attend a union meeting, or simply to listen to a lecture. That always means overcoming the desire for tranquility. This is the new kind of penance demanded of the men and women of our time.

When it comes to the actual work of forming a team, I would like to speak particularly to the women teachers. It is always a little daunting to make statements about women. Anybody can make his little joke in private or tell his off-colour story; in public, very few go beyond some slight allusion or stupid remark. For women make public opinion, and that is infinitely to be feared. The old saying sums up the wisdom of the people: what woman wants, God wants. The great Tolstoi himself avows his holy fear of women when he writes to his friend Gorki, "When I am halfway into the tomb, I'll say what I think about women and quickly shut the tombstone down on me." Last year an article in *Chatelaine* asked, "Do Men Fear Women?" Of course they do, above all in this matriarchal North America of ours. Nevertheless I'm going to say what I have to say, with the desperate courage of those who have nothing to lose because they have renounced everything.

Women make up the immense majority of Quebec's teaching personnel. The 1957-58 Report of the Superintendent of Public Instruction gives the following figures: 20,219 women lay teachers out of a total of 34,546 religious and lay teachers, both men and women. They are then nearly two-thirds of the total. But as to length of service, the situation is reversed; men have an average of 15.7 years of teaching, against 8.5 for women. These figures are for the whole Province, and include all the women. In fact, if we deduct a few dozen women who make a definite career of teaching, and average the rest, it appears that the women teachers average only about five years in the occupation. The great majority of the feminine personnel changes every four or five years.

These two factors, the female majority and the short duration of their stay in the profession bring notable consequences. Among them is the women's lack of interest in the profound and radical problems of the profession. Salary problems are urgent, but they are not deep. A really deep problem is, for instance, promotion by merit. The result of this composition of the teaching force shows up in the behaviour of the teachers' unions. Their long term policies cannot help being affected by this demographic imbalance. Don't misunderstand me, I'm not going back to the age of the cave man. Women as a separate class are becoming more and more important. The movement for their emancipation is irreversible; it is normal and good when it comes about naturally according to the innate will of nature and the real needs of society.

We have no reason to deplore the advent of Woman in History, however silent she has been hitherto. Until now, History has been made by men exclusively. Considering what they have done with it, it is hard to see why women shouldn't take a hand. Far from dispatching them back into the shadows, let us rather urge them to hasten their political maturity. I'm not joking when I say these things. Listen to these extracts from a manifesto of the *Jeunesse Ouvrière Catholique* [Catholic Workers Youth Movement] published as recently as February, 1960.

The problem of women's participation in their unions is even more pressing than that of the men's. Recent figures from the National Syndicates indicate that out of 100,000 members, only 15,000 are women. A good part of the young working women who do belong pay their dues but take no active part. The difficulty they have in expressing them-

selves in public, the small share of time that is granted
them at meetings, hinder them from claiming their rights,
from being true leaders in their professional organizations.

A very small percentage of the women who work is
unionized at all, and still smaller is the number who take
an active part. For psychological reasons, a woman says
to herself that she will be working only a few years, and
she doesn't see the importance of joining. Women are
interested in the union when it is time to sign a wage
contract or ask for a raise, but they ignore or neglect to
consult their union about bettering their working conditions, though that is the only way to act effectively. In a
television interview of René Lévesque's *Point de Mire* after
the '56 elections, the answers given by the women he
questioned showed they knew next to nothing about
politics and that their votes were not based on any serious
considerations. 'I voted for X because my father always
voted that way — I voted for such and such a man because
he looked so kind—'

These findings do not apply especially to the women
teachers; they are more intellectually and politically developed than the adolescents whose behaviour we have
just described. But it is still a fact that women teachers do
need to be more conscious of their social responsibilities,
to take deliberate steps toward political advancement.
They will act more quickly and to better advantage if they
are more fully aware of what they are doing, if they are
able to act with understanding and sincerity.

For the women to form a team then implies the as-
sumption of certain vital obligations; perhaps it implies
greater self-sacrifice than for the men. I think that the
most urgent task for them is to familiarize themselves
with parliamentary procedure and legal machinery, with
the correct democratic functioning of their association.
They will have to get into the habit of looking at things in
large and universal perpective, in the perspective of the
future.

Of course everybody, men as well as women in our profession, must make an effort to grow up politically. If I

make a special appeal to the women, it is because of those two reasons, their preponderance in numbers and the short stay they make in the career. They can, if they choose, dominate the politics of their association but their brief acquaintance with it implies the risk that they will enforce an ill-thought-out policy, or will make no use at all of their power, which would be no less an evil.

One last point that I want to consider is that of vertical relations. Taken as a group, teachers include not only the rank and file, but also Superiors, a hierarchy of them, and a hierarchy arranged in a tight structure. I have the impression that our relations with authority are not in general too healthy. They have need of an airing. The dull heavy oppression that has weighed on us so long has at last squeezed from us some feeble protests. At the moment they are feeble indeed, but they will grow. Now that a breach has been made it will be widened, and freedom will, I hope, return to us through that breach.

Fear is unhealthy. And God knows that we are all a-fraid, afraid of each other. I know some professors who live in terror of their union officials. How can we educate the young, inspire our poor small nation, if we ourselves are timid and subservient? We have no idea, you have no idea, of the wonderful liberty which Jesus Christ came to bestow on us. This liberty is not insolence or anarchy. Every sensible man knows that a society needs leaders, but to honour a leader doesn't mean to crawl to him.

We are all men, and men are made to stand upright. It's time to take the axe to this fetich of authority that has been imposed on us, a fetich that we perpetuate by servility and stupidity. We needn't revolt, we only need to regain a little human dignity. Blessed are the peacemakers, says the Gospel. Just so, those whom the Gospel declares blessed are the ones who make peace, as one makes new land, fighting against the rocks, the roots, the quackgrass. To be peaceful doesn't mean to be asleep and indifferent.

St.Thomas Aquinas associates the gift of wisdom with the beatitude of the peacemakers. Wisdom is the active desire to partake of the spiritual. The sweetest fruit that wisdom can perceive from far away, is the fruit of liberty. It would move heaven and earth to make it grow, this fruit of liberty. Let's be done with this fear. It's now or never, the Province of Quebec is on the eve of a decisive move.

We teachers ought to be aware of this movement which is beginning, we ought to be eager to play a leading part in the shake-up that's on the way. To apply to our position an allegory of Mounier's, let's say the doorkeeper of History turns away pitilessly "those warped beings who travel through life askew with downcast eyes, those lame moral hair-splitters, pious shaky-kneed, sappy heroes, slick babes, faded virgins, pots of boredom, sacks of syllogisms, shadows of shadows."

We might as well admit that a pernickety and ever-present bureaucracy which follows us watchfully step by step, obliging us to play the role of janitor, insurance agent, tax collector, freezing us in routine jobs where we spend our time making little blue and red marks in notebooks, recording temperatures, and all that nonsense, has emasculated and dulled us, making us into fussy, lifeless automatons. But now the Province is moving. Don't let that move go on without us. Let us preside over that resurgence of the French Canadian which is coming fast. In his book, *The Future of Man*, Teilhard de Chardin speaks of education as the chief factor in evolution. As our work goes on in the field of education, let us be conscious of working within the current of evolution. Let us be proud, knowing that we take part in the work of Creation, of all Creation which in groaning awaits, St. Paul assures us, the manifestation of the Children of God.

All the stairs we climb behind the lines of our students, all the rules of grammar we repeat, all the problems we solve, all the pains we take, let us do them in the knowledge that we hasten that manifestation of the Children of God, for which all Creation longs. And the Children of God, let us say once more, are free. God loves only liberty. "When one has known what it is to be loved freely," says Péguy in *The Mystery of the Holy Innocents,* "submissiveness has no flavour. When one has known the love of free men, the prostrations of slaves mean nothing." Let us then give Him free men; let us make free men, and for that let us free ourselves.

The instrument of all liberation is knowledge. Here once more we encounter the stern appeal to quality.

CHAPTER II

LETTER TO A YOUNG BROTHER

The man who is writing to you now is not himself a very old Brother, though some happenings in his life have speeded up his inner history and contributed to ripen him in his springtime. (He flatters himself complacently.) Sounds like Jean-Jacques Rousseau talking, doesn't it? Don't worry, I'll soon quit this confessional style.

You were telling me the other day that life in the Posts* raises terrible doubts in your mind. You knew, you said, several companions who seemed very sound when they were living in the training schools, and who, after a year or two in the Posts, have left the Order. You wonder what caused these desertions, what difficulties they could have encountered to discourage them so.

The life of a teaching Brother in a Post is tough, no doubt about it, and often very wearisome. I will not hide my embarrassment from you. I have been a young Brother myself: how could one dodge that stage? But when the time comes to talk about it, I don't seem to be able to. What did I suffer from? What were my great hardships? Were they caused by men or circumstances? By the work,

---

* The teaching Orders in Quebec, both men's and women's, when requested, will send groups of their members to run schools under the control of school commissions in towns away from their own community centers. These groups are "posts," or "missions."

or by the community life? Or by myself? How can I sort out all that?

I realize I have to begin with some pretty strong assertions. I have some venerable thinkers against me, a lot of piety, some solid clichés, and above all, fear. No matter, here we go. "If a writer is so cautious that he never writes anything that can be criticized, he will never write anything worth reading. But if you want to help the world to rise, make up your mind once for all to write things that certain mediocre men will condemn." A monk, Thomas Merton, said that. I will tell you, to begin with, that regularity makes life easier. We commit ourselves once for all to a regular schedule through laziness and a meanness of soul. Doubtless I surprise you. You have always been told, and you begin to find out for yourself, that it costs a lot to be regular. I shan't contradict that. I only tell you that most men are willing to pay a heavy price for security and a good conscience. In an environment like ours, to be regular is the shortest way to a good reputation and a clear conscience, to peace and all the blessings of earth and heaven. Nobody tells you that it is perhaps also the surest way to avoid all risks and stifle all vitality. I have long observed that the most regular among us, the most consistently regular, the most official in their regularity, are also the most superficial, the most dried up, the farthest removed from their fellow human beings. Doubtless they believe that being distant from men is enough to bring them close to God. I can't help thinking here of a certain inspector whom St. Exupéry in *Night Flight* contrasts with his hero leader: "A regulation established by Rivière was, for Rivière, a means of knowing his men; but for Robineau there existed no more than a knowledge of the regulation."

I add here, so that you may see in what spirit I write these lines, that our most valuable regulations are those that regulate the least. The articles on the spirit of faith, on humility and penitence, are easily defendable, but you won't be praised for regularity if you do no more than practise the spirit of faith. Don't expect me to say that the important thing for me is to "pass for regular."

We shall never know to what extent rationalism has contaminated western thought. Cartesianism didn't begin with Descartes, but with the monks who invented clocks, because it is well known that God has his habits and it is the proper thing to pray to him at certain hours. Has it been impressed on you enough that rationalism is a manifestation of the security instinct? We leave nothing to chance, we distrust the unknown, we try to introduce regularities,which can be known, wherever it can be done. So we tend to reduce the margin of liberty, which coincides with the margin of life. Life brings the unpredictable, and only by faith can the unpredictable be endured. But faith is uncomfortable. It is a trial, a great trial, the trial of our first parents. God asked them to be content with not knowing everything at once, but Satan arrived, saying "Come come, you shall be like gods, sure of all things, knowing good and evil." They swapped faith for arithmetic. Mathematics came into the world, Descartes appeared on the horizon. Adam was the first of the rationalists.As for Eve, she wanted security first of all.

Am I not afraid that these remarks will be interpreted as advice to take it easy? The scale for weighing things of the mind is just as sensitive as that for weighing bodies. "You talk about regularity making life easy but I think irregularity could make it easy too. If we must choose between facilities, why not pick the first one — after all, it's not as widespread as the other?" The objection is weighty. I can answer only that a man must set forth what he believes to be the truth, without being bothered if his words are "twisted by rascals to trouble fools."

And then you will ask impatiently, for it must seem to you that I am not very consistent at this point, "Shall I be regular in my life?" Why of course you will be regular as long as you can and maybe a little longer, for as the proverb says, Weariness makes a long job. I don't mean I want you to have a totally unreliable disposition, one that can't be relied on. I approve regularity, military regularity, but I intend you to have it while realizing that it amounts to very little.

Since you are a young Brother, when I speak of your colleagues I am necessarily speaking of those older than you. When I say "aged Brother," you will read "someone older than I." The question is, how should you behave toward them? To honour all men, as St. Benoit directed, ought to be your rule. Jolly familiarity and whacks on the back don't bring men closer, they blot them out. St. Exupéry said somewhere that the man who is not given consideration, kills. I know that many of the young Brothers complain of the lack of encouragement from the older men, but it is their own attitude which is to blame. The elderly Brother who does not receive from the young the marks of respect to which he has a right, reacts with indifference, hostility, distrust.

These older men, unless they are saints who have become detached from everything, most of all from themselves, suffer from the mediocrity of their social standing in the community. Everybody can't be a Director. We need only about thirty Directors. The rest are anonymous foot-travelers. Soon enough, a Brother feels left aside. Soon enough, he sees what his life is going to be like, that of an obscure sentinel. He knows he is all through with promotions, that he is settled for good, that he will never be more than a humble day labourer in his field. Provided that he is on hand for his class, nobody notices him or pays any attention to him. If he doesn't call attention to himself by some misconduct, he will pass his whole life in obscurity. Nobody, unless it is St. John of the Cross, likes being ignored and taken for granted as next to nothing. Here the young Brothers can help a lot; by asking advice of an older Brother, by showing him consideration, a young Brother can pull him out of his slump, he can revive him.

An elderly Brother will always feel a lasting gratitude for such consideration.

Don't say I'm preaching Dale Carnegie stuff and his potted recipes. I'm not showing you tricks to help you get something out of people with a pretence of friendship or some ingenious falsehood. I want you to value sincerely the experience of these old Brothers. I want you to ask their advice because you really appreciate their value and their wisdom. Remember always that their greatest merit and their highest qualification is that they have endured.

Only a man's occupation saves him. To earn one's living is the first commandment and the first charity. Even before the Fall, God had ordered man to work. Your work is to teach your classes. Don't call it a vocation or an apostolate. We have come near dying of all these big words and all this self-pity. Call it a trade. Humble words are first in the kingdom of thought, as humble men are first in the Kingdom of God.

Let your occupation come first in your life. God and men are not loved abstractly, they are loved in and by one's work. Consequently — and I ask you to weigh my words as I do myself — if at some moment you are too tired to do your job properly and also attend to your community duties, be ruthless about the latter and attend to your job. If, at some moment, you need the hour set apart for religious study to prepare a lesson in mathematics for your class, ask permission and prepare your course. Your first duty is to teach your class. Here the little imp who never leaves me and who reads over my shoulder, laughs in my ear — if you need your hour of religious study to prepare your lesson in religion, don't hesitate, use it. That's what it's for.

Don't let the Pharisees trouble your conscience. I speak of them often, because the religious life is the most congenial place in the world for those vermin to propagate and spread. They differ from common vermin in that ordinary rats keep out of sight, while the Pharisees occupy the limelight. Don't be unhappy or feel guilty when you make those necessary shifts in routine, don't even talk about them to anybody, for your work should require all your solicitude and all your energy. The rest is dross, pious or not, or mischief-making not worthy of attention.

But do the young Brothers really like their work? I confess to some doubts. They no longer talk shop among themselves; they talk sport or books. It is a disquieting sign. In my time, we talked shop and nothing else, and even now, after several years, our work is still our principal subject of conversation.

St. Exupéry based his conclusion that work unites men on his experience as an airplane pilot. Perhaps you will have noticed that ours does not always work that way. In his occupation, he fought the elements; each man depended on the other for life itself, not just reputation or prestige. In our work we fight the passions, we fight laziness, boredom, mediocrity. Soon we oppose passion to passion. Each of us works alone, and as our whole spirit is engaged in our work, our whole personality is shaken by any threat against it. The upshot is that we suffer from rivalries, jealousies, all the gamut of social emotions. So it often happens that our work sets us one against the other. It's best to face that fact and not be too scandalized by it. The remedy here is not to contribute to the little meannesses that encumber our daily task, but to be ourselves openhearted, clearheaded and flexible. The joy of one won't become the joy of his neighbours all at once, nor the success of one the happiness of all, as happens naturally in a family, but again I must repeat that we are not a family of flesh and blood.

Everyone knows what I have just said, each of us has had proof of it, but what does that matter? It is always necessary to deny these things officially, isn't it? Always

put on the official optimism, like General Gamelin in June
of 1940. Two days before the catastrophe everything was
just fine. You have only to read the *Mémoires de guerre* by
General de Gaulle. Those who prophesy deluges are ridi-
culed or sawed in two, like Noah or Isaiah. Those who see
and formulate the problems that others refuse to see must
expect to be taken for cranks, phonies, or hotheads.

I have not yet asked the fundamental question, which
is: Do you like young people? In our work you have to
like young people, or you can't survive. The quarrels with
your colleagues, the Director's lack of understanding, the
daily routine, however much they annoy you, are easily
borne if you like the young and find happiness in being
with them. You may say, "But how could one not like
young people?" Look out! As long as it's only a matter of
liking the freshness, the spontaneity, the generosity of
youth, all goes well enough. Everyone wishes what is good.
But for us in our position to love youth imposes a heavier
burden. We must love them as Maria Chapdelaine's father
loved the land, to make something of it. "Five times since
his youth he had taken up land, built a house, a stable and
a barn, carved a prosperous holding out of the woods, and
five times he had sold this property in order to begin again
farther north, because he was at once discouraged and lost
all interest when the first rough labour was done, once
neighbours arrived and the country was opened up. A few
men understood him; others found him brave but foolish,
and repeated that he ought to settle down somewhere, now
that he and his family could take their ease."

We also must work the land, cultivate the intelligence,
sow the seed year after year, and never see the harvest, or
almost never. Do we love the young enough to be content
forever with future joys? That's the whole question. We
have to have Samuel Chapdelaine's passion for the land.
One of the finest sayings ever to come from the heart of
man is that of William the Silent: "It is not necessary to

have hope in order to undertake a task, or to succeed in order to persevere." I think we can make our own this proud protest, though sometimes we can take to ourselves a little hope.

The joys of the harvest are for others, for others the durable and definite influences. "Sculptors of smoke," (Montherlant) we play only an episodic and doubtful role, and the kind of benefits we offer are neither the most urgent nor the most apparent — nor the most welcome. I recall the comparison which Lalanne made in his almost unknown book, *Theophrastus' Last Voyage to Lilliput*. He said something like this, "All teachers are subject to two judgments from their pupils, the first during the time they are with them, the second several years later. Usually they are found guilty in the first trial, but the best of them are acquitted in the second."

Obviously this is something of a caricature, but Lalanne's meaning is easy enough to see. I wonder, then, if you love youth enough to accept from it in the time that you serve, levity always, indifference often, hostility sometimes? Is your love big enough to be satisfied with an eventual, posthumous acquittal? That's the nub of the whole question. The picture I draw may seem unduly one-sided to you. Of course what I have been saying is not the whole story, nor does it satisfy your dreams. Maybe halfway? Who was it said that the truth is like a spark that flames for a moment between the positive and negative poles, the electric arc? You will grind out the grist from all that I have said and from your own dreams, which will contain the essentials.

To the extent that you are sentimental — and who is not? — you will find the life of the Posts rather barren, the Brothers rough, and your heartfelt desires unfulfilled. You see I don't sweeten the pill, I am more inclined to make it bitter. It is true that the life is tough enough, and you feel it more at certain times. Sundays for instance, are proverbially dismal. It is not only my personal impression. I shall come back to this point later. If I were not speaking to a younger man, I would not bother with the two matters I am about to take up, but as it is I will mention them. The harshness of our life will strike you most acutely in times of illness, on birthdays and similar occasions. I hasten to explain, for I know that I'm not being very clear.

When I say illness, I don't mean anything serious. Of course if you fall gravely ill, you will receive all the attention and all the care you could wish for. Besides, you will have the advantage that your illness will be a catastrophe for no one but yourself. No woman or child will suffer from the failure of earning power which a severe illness entails, nor from the grief that comes from the illness of someone near and dear. I refer rather to slight illnesses. Suppose you have the flu — that can happen to any Christian. You have to stay in your room for two or three days. So, you are left alone. And you feel abandoned. At home your mother or your big sister would have petted you, spoiled you, tucked you into bed. Here in the Post, there's none of that. They know you are in no danger, and that's that. You find this very hard. You are wrong. You forget that your colleagues have their own work to do; they wouldn't know how to take care of you if they wanted to, and after all a male is a male. I would not hark back to this matter if I had not before now received confidences that confirm my belief that more than one departure has been decided on in such circumstances. I wouldn't say such a situation would decide everything, but it might be the last straw.

At home, birthdays are events. Here, they are likely to pass in silence. Or perhaps you receive some diploma or other, an event for you. At home there would be congratulations and rejoicings. Here nobody will take any notice, or if there are any congratulations, they are purely formal. And you, who would have liked to be a big shot in the community for a day, you find yourself right back where you were, the youngest Brother.

I give these examples in detail, because it is just as well to be prepared. If you expect to find an atmosphere of family warmth in the Posts, you will be disappointed. The Posts are big or little workshops. You are there to work or to educate yourself, which is still work. There are a few official good times, like the Christmas holidays if your director is capable; there are a few unofficial good times which you will make for yourself when you learn how. But on the whole you have to learn that nobody in particular is concerned with you on the Post. If you were married, your wife would be there. As you went toward home, you would be saying to yourself that someone was waiting for you, that someone would know your step. Here no one waits for you. So be it. The religious life is not arranged for the temporal happiness of its followers. No one makes a vow of happiness.

But let me soften the prospect a little. You will gradually find friends, in the community. You will find them if you deserve them, if you are friendly yourself, friends whose like you could never find outside. Men who, like you, have given up everything, who have the same ideals, the same training, who encounter the same difficulties. There is just as good a chance to know great men in the community as in the world outside. We should be fair. Personally I feel that the strongest human link that binds me to the community is the friendship of a few men.

I'd like to name some of them. Let people say what they please, say that the names are of no interest, say that they're all unknown. I don't care, I'm going to name some. Greetings, Louis-Grégoire, Paul-Gérard, Rosario, Donat; greetings, Jean Gérard, Rosaire-Raymond, Armand-Benoit, Sylvio-Alfred, Pierre-Xavier, Jacques-Lucien, Firmin-Marie, Henri-Georges, Alexis-Marie. Greetings, my old Brothers. Where would I ever find men like you? How ever

leave you? How ever abandon such a treasure of friendship? How ever forget you, old trees set out ten or fifteen
years ago and now beginning to give shade. I do not want
to speak at random, I want to name you to anchor what I
have said, to incarnate, to humanize what I have said with
the real names of real men. I did not deserve you, I have
you just the same. Greetings, my old Brothers, greetings.

Will you be happy or unhappy? The question is wrongly
put. There is no choice except between happiness and un-
happiness. Between the two, there may be greatness. You
will have opportunities to be great, that is, useful to others.
Greatness will not be lacking in your life. Only try not to
fail when the time for greatness comes.

*　*　*

Half the human race is of the female sex: I don't need
to tell you that. It is pretty hard to ignore that fact, and
hard likewise to ignore the inclination that bears us toward
women. Here and anywhere, man and beast are not far
apart. Then there are women who are both beautiful and
kind. We have pledged ourselves to live without women.
We have been educated far from them, too far perhaps —
not physically, for that is a matter of strict necessity, but
intellectually. Our training in this respect as in several
other ways is rather unrealistic. In the Posts, however, we
are no longer so very far from women.

Do not be too alarmed when you feel within your heart
this emptiness, this sudden pang of human love. If you
would deal with it, begin by being clear about it. Woman
is part of the whole man. Alone, you are essentially incomplete. You incarnate only imperfectly the idea of man.
Plato speaks of man, of certain men, as beings cut in two,
wandering through the world in search of their other half.
The inclination toward human love is not a caprice, or any-

thing transitory. A man alone is mutilated. Woman, says Genesis, is the half of man, made not from his rib, but from his whole side. Don't despise yourself because you feel this impulse toward women, admit it to yourself. Don't try to make believe that the grapes are sour. "I do not wish you to degrade your treasures through cowardice, in order to regret them less" (St. Exupéry). The sour grape technique works only once. The moment always comes when you have to dig up a deeper response or break. Do not despise yourself when you find that the love of God is not enough, that the plainest of the pretty girls interests you more than the Virgin Mary. It's normal. Sanctity is a fruit of autumn, not of spring, with very rare exceptions. A man has to walk long in darkness and confusion to reach the serene heights. Despise rather the too rapid peace; it is not real. Despise the peace that is the result of capitulation, deserve slowly the peace of the conqueror. The quick and easy solace is to rush into human love, or still worse into the ignoble expedients which I will not name, but which you can guess. I have a great desire to say to you, "You have this impulse, recognize it for what it is; do not be ashamed, and endure."

And will that go on for a long time? Long enough. Peace on these grounds is called sanctity and nothing else. I don't suppose anyone ever told you that the religious life was easy. It is a high and somber adventure, an adventure for men, and only men succeed in it.

No one can hope to love God as he would love a woman, nor the Holy Virgin as he would love his little neighbour. That would really be too simple. If it were like that the Orders would be refusing postulants, which is hardly the case, as you know.

As to the Holy Virgin, however, it is a little different, for she is a woman, a beautiful woman, a fresh young girl. She is in Heaven in body and spirit. I suggest to you that a normal man can succeed in loving the Virgin Mary in the way a man can love his fiancée even when separated from her. In the heart of the desert, says St. Exupéry, a man can be rich with the image of his well-beloved. In the heart of our lives, we can be rich with the image and the presence of the Virgin Mary. And we have an advantage over the young man who is parted from his beloved — we can speak to the Holy Virgin and our words will be heard. Even our thoughts will be heard, and every loving action. The young man thinks of his well-beloved, he speaks to her in his secret heart, but his words do not reach her, and he knows it. But if we speak to the Holy Virgin, in the silence of our love, our words reach her. She knows when we speak to her, when we think of her. The special litanies to the Virgin take on a rich meaning here, for in these litanies we give her the finest compliments that overflowing hearts have dreamed of for many centuries. A whole psychology of women is to be found in the litanies to the Holy Virgin, Faithful Virgin, Prudent Virgin, Mother of Good Counsel, Consoler, Mother, Little Sister of the Human Race.

* * *

Before everything else, you will cultivate your own mind. Culture is the foundation of a man's life. Alain says the Latinist is never bored. There is an inexhaustible pleasure in culture, and the ways to it are always open. Find your happiness within yourself. Find within yourself a wealth that you can take with you wherever you go, a wealth that no one can take away from you unless he destroys you as a man. Your culture will be your own as long as you live. Cultivate your mind, and for that, learn to read. Duhamel says that a reading people is a people saved. I would gladly say the same thing of a young Brother. If boredom is the exhaustion of courage, one can say that culture is the cure for boredom at its roots. The Latinist is never bored, even on Sunday. You think I have a grudge against Sundays? No, not really, but others have told me they have. They will read my answer to them here.

You will think perhaps that I am terribly profane, almost impious. Just think, I haven't yet spoken of the Blessed Founder of our Order, of prayer, of daily communion, of novenas. It's true, I haven't. I think, with Alain, that it's best not to resort too early to the sovereign remedies — not that I think they might fail, but lest you might not be equal to them. To begin with mysticism and get sick of it leaves the victim hopeless, but to begin with human culture is almost surely to go on to higher things. First of all then depend on your own intelligence.

Depend on your muscles too. I like to see a young Brother strong, physically strong. Illness and physical weakness complicate everything. They do nobody any good, unless it is the saints. St. François de Sales is often quoted, "Better keep up your strength more than is necessary than break it down more than is necessary, for it can always be diminished but not always repaired when you want it. Better accept the penance of labour than of fasting." Then be strong. I don't say be a sportsman, above all not a television sportsman. For instance, be a good walker, the most terrific walker on earth. Walking exercises the whole man. Lay out for yourself a simple program of physical culture and stick to it. But, as I said, first of all, walk. "Participate in the dignity of this uniquely human act, walking" (Lanza del Vasto).

Try always to think of your body as an instrument. The body exists for the soul, to be the instrument of the soul. It is to be expected that an instrument will become blunted with use. You must not hope for eternal youth, you must accept weariness and aging. I have seen that it is possible to develop a sort of aristocratic and tender friendship for your body, the kind of attachment that one feels for some useful and familiar object. "Know your body. It is something that comes to you from outside, one object among others, which you can use as a sounding lead to dip into the outside world. Among all the other things, it is the only key you have to the meaning of all the rest. All creation has its echo in your body like the noise of the sea in a conch shell" (Lanza del Vasto).

Body, my old brother, you have often failed me, but all the same we shall arrive together at the gates of the Kingdom of God. You, bent, harassed, broken, I newer than the morning. Soon you will recover the qualities that you have worn yourself out to gain for me, the qualities for which you have slowly bartered yourself, clarity, agility, subtlety, stoicism. Those are heavy words which indicate awkwardly the marvellous realizations that await us, of which we have sung. With what enthusiasm and what faith, thou and I, *exspecto resurrectionem mortuorum* — I await the resurrection of the dead.

* * *

You say to me in your letter that you have known comrades who have left our ranks after a short time in a Post, and you ask why. I have pointed out some of the difficulties and the snares in the way, such as the stifling daily round, the erudite obstacle of the Rule, squabbles with one's colleagues, the unavoidable misunderstandings with the Director, disgust with the work, boredom, the longing for happiness on the human scale. All that really explains nothing. "The motives alleged for departures or abandonments of the vocation, are very often only pretexts," declares a 1958 circular. "The real cause is to be sought elsewhere and often goes back several years. The trouble is not so much in external circumstances, such as the other brothers and the superiors, as in the spirit within, weakness, pride, lack of generosity, absence of a truly interested religious spirit."

These are severe strictures, to which I must nevertheless agree. Peter and Andrew accepted on the spot the invitation of the Master; the rich young man refused. That's all there is to it. He who goes away sorrowful is the rich young man. Perhaps not sorrowful right away. Julien Green describes somewhere the relief he experienced the day he decided to refuse the call to the religious life. He felt at first as if he had shed a heavy garment. Our pleasures make poor guides. But listen to a well-known critic:

> Green's first impression after making his great refusal was an immense inner relief; a weight had been taken off him, the weight of the Cross. The lesson here is precious; it is psychologically simple to imagine that the first emotion of the Christian who refuses something God has asked of him will be terror and anguish; on the contrary it is liberation, a feeling of regaining possession of oneself. It is the life of God which is difficult, it is that which crucifies. The joy it gives is so profound that it is found only beyond the suffering, in the night of faith. The first emotion of Adam after the Fall was that of entering upon the possession of the world and of himself. The sinner lives at a superficial level, while the evil that has been done goes deep into a zone where ordinary psychology cannot penetrate. St. Gregory says wisely, 'Material goods seem the most precious of all when you have them not; on the contrary, spiritual goods, so long as one does not enjoy them, seem unreal. Material pleasures, once experienced, reveal only after a long time the satiety they conceal, while spiritual realities, once possessed, are seen to be inexhaustible.'

> > (Charles Moeller, *Christianity and the Literature of the Twentieth Century*).

I'm not done yet. All that I've just said or quoted puts the whole burden of responsibility on the shoulders of the young Brother. It is not forbidden, though it may be rather touchy to put into words, to suggest that faults may be found within the Community itself. If the lower orders are not entirely without sin, it is hard to see how the superiors as a group can escape it. Is it possible to assume that the superiors have never, as superiors, made a mistake? Who can say that the history of the teaching Brothers is all that it ought to have been? Historically, have we never been at fault? Have we not failed in our mission, at least in part? Is there nothing but positive accomplishment in our past? Any sensible man can see that we are not without blame. We have made errors of policy, we have lacked foresight, we have not always met challenges as we should have. I know these remarks will appear pretentious to some, pretentious and worse than that, insolent. Pretentious my eye! If we have made mistakes, the lower ranks are not alone to blame. If, generally speaking, we have to attribute some mistakes to authority as such, we are compelled by the same token to absolve the rank and file.

When I speak here of authority, I mean also certain conventions, certain characteristics, of our community life. So far as I know, these arrangements are invented and maintained by the authorities. If the prescriptions are inadequate or even harmful, the authorities and not the rank and file are to blame. You can see I speak of these matters with fear and trembling, as befits one who seeks salvation, even though it seems to me I have some backing for my views. Such as Pius XII, "It is possible that some points of the routine, some directives, which are not simple applications of the Rule, some customs which used to be suited to the conditions of another time, but which at present only complicate the educational work, ought to be changed to fit new circumstances."

The young, indeed, adjust poorly to out of date and ancient rules. An older man, because he is experienced, may have succeeded in adapting himself to the regulations, or in adapting them a bit to his needs. But a young man....

Canon Leclercq, who is not on the Index, says in his *Religious Vocation* that it is not words but the realities which they represent that we have to fear. If we don't say them, History will say them for us, and History is pitiless. I think that in investigating departures from the Order, without prejudice to the paragraph we cited from the December, 1958 circular, which furnished the principal reasons, we may find some explanation for these same departures in this dislike of the old ways.

But why hint at this to the young Brothers, someone will ask. Are they not already prone enough to criticise? Why furnish them new weapons? I find they certainly are ready enough to criticise, and I consequently avoid handing them new weapons. But I know that stupid, unhealthy, depressing, constipated criticism always comes from incomplete knowledge or cloudy thinking, never from a thorough analysis. To examine the problems and state them realistically is a manly and positive move.

Don't think you have done much for authority when you have simply denied any possibility of error. Why, some of the Popes have made mistakes; at one time or another the Episcopate of a country could commit an error; who is to say that our Directors have never made the least mistake, that all their decisions were excellent, their judgments uniformly sound? Me, I think it is not sacrilegious to think the contrary. You don't destroy authority by saying it is human, and so liable to error. The surest way to destroy it is to insist on idolatrous respect. In time idols waste away. A durable respect for authority must be based on common sense. The truth doesn't foster illusion and conceit. Two months in a Post will strangely disillusion a young Brother who has been taught to look on his Director as the replica of God-the-Father. He would be spared the disappointments which turn into cynicism if he were told at the outset that human attempts to realize the Kingdom of God are as poor and pitiful as human attempts to conceive of God. Our institutions are as deficient as our ideas. That's no reason to quit trying; it is the precondition of a farsighted and efficient effort.

This long digression has not made me forget my principal idea, which is this: a man must carry his reasons for living a long time before they carry him. At first everything is only an unfolding in the night, a freedom won in anguish.

ENVOI

And so that, my dear young Brother, is what I had to say to you — nothing very new or very revolutionary. How far have I been able to answer you, how useful has my advice been to you? I don't know. At the end of this unintentionally long letter, I am still moved to wonder if I have succeeded in helping you. Anyhow, that was the intention, for to help other men is all there is in life. Love is just the highest name for pity. And it is a good thing, isn't it, for a man to have some place in the world where he can find pity; without pity life's not bearable.

I remember a telephone call that I had a few years ago. One of the men who drives the bus from Quebec wanted to report to the school office that a student who rode with him every day had left his school bag and his books in the bus. I made a note of it and thanked him. Before hanging up, he asked me if I knew a certain Brother, who used to teach at the school. He seemed very pleased to have the few bits of news I gave him.

Afterwards, I began to think this over. Men need some men they can tie to, men they can trust once for all. They need to know that in spite of all the changes, there are some islands of faithfulness and affirmation of eternal truths. The greatest service that we can render to the men of our time is to affirm the absolute. The denial of the absolute is our great modern sickness. Men need to know that there are some men who do not change.

Men find it good to know that there are still the Brothers. As pupils, they know such and such a one. Afterwards, they embark on their lives — what is commonly called Life. They have developed, they have changed, they have known many disappointments, they know now that man is not happy. At forty, one knows that man is not happy. One day, it occurs to them to inquire if Brother So-and-so is still there, he who used to talk to them about religion, about Jesus Christ and the Blessed Mary, about Christian values, and — who knows? — even about democracy. What security then for them to learn that this man is still at his post, unchanged, everlasting! Then he wasn't fooling them. All his words suddenly become validated, retroactively. Their values crystallize.

I will close by quoting St. Exupéry once more, the only one of our contemporary writers touched by glory, not merely celebrity. As the light of a star sometimes comes to us long after it is burned out, his warmth may reach you now. We never know for whom we write. "We are the few who watch over men, to whom the stars give answer. We are the few on high, who have set our choice on God. Bearing with us the burden of the city, we are fixed in place, scourged by the frozen wind that falls like an icy cloak from the stars."

With our choice set on God and the Holy Mary.

POSTSCRIPT

The other day I was travelling on a bus with a colleague. He sat with a person who appeared to be at the very least a Canon, while I found a place two rows ahead. The first part of the trip passed in interplanetary silence. Maurice Chevalier assures us that when a marquis meets another marquis, they tell each other stories about marquises. But when a Brother meets a Canon, they don't tell each other anything. Nevertheless the Canon had something he wanted to get off his chest. Addressing my friend at last, he asked him if he knew Brother Anonymous. "There he is in front of you," replied my colleague, like a good stool-pigeon. The Canon thereupon went off in a tirade about my flamboyant language and theological errors. My friend defended me valiantly — an awfully good sort, that guy.

In debarking from the bus — can one, yes or no, debark from a bus? — the Canon held out his hand to me and I asked him his name. He would not tell me. I insisted, he refused. I insisted and finally found out. (Later my friend completed his dossier for me by telling me he was the principal of a normal school at L'Islet and that he had studied at Rome.) After stating his name, the Prelate cautioned me to be prudent and patted me paternally on the arm. "Be careful, or you'll run into trouble," he said.

"With whom?" I inquired.

"Be careful," he repeated. It was all he said.

In thirty seconds of conversation with a complete unknown, we had exhausted the tactics of certain Quebec clergy — the paternal pat and the unctuous threat.

* * *

I make jokes, I play the clown, I pass out insults, of

course. But that's not all. The main thing is that I love the people hereabouts, the French Canadians of my Province. I am so much one of them, rooted in this land. I beg everyone to believe me that I honestly don't hate anybody — I know I don't deserve it, but I still beg you to believe me. I am not a rebel. I usually write in very good humor, except when I feel an attack of indigestion coming on, which happens to me once a week. Then I go on a diet — seven consecutive meals of Kellogg's "Special K", you know, the box with the big red "K".

What I want to do is to create a demand for air. I want people around here to breathe freely. Personally, I have never been a victim of injustice; personally, I breathe all right. I have no grudge to settle with anybody. I am not an unlucky man. An unlucky man has no business meddling in philosophy. Seriously, I am rather lucky. First I had the good luck — I say it without irony — to be born into a poor family. We have always been poor at home, close to misery. Truly wretched at times. I used to study my lessons by the light of a kerosene lamp, for the simple reason that my parents hadn't the money to hitch onto Saguenay Power. When the Brothers picked me out, they had to pay my way through the seminary, clothe and teach me for charity. They have done that for thousands of French Canadians, though not many know it.

Then I got tuberculosis. I came out of it as best I could, badly marked by the experience, but full of the Old Nick. This interminable illness was a blessing, for it gave me time to reflect. I was humiliated in the only fashion that really counts, in my physical strength. You can always deny that you have no sense, no taste, no culture — you can simply refuse to face it. But you can't ignore being out of breath.

I got the chance to know some wonderful men and women at the hospital. I met real French Canadians there. I also had an opportunity to read a little, and I even knew a Jesuit to whom I owe a great deal.

What I want now is to express through my words the generations of silent ones from whom I have sprung. My father does not know how to read and write. It is not his fault — at fourteen he was working in the lumber camps. Is that terrible enough? Has he endured enough, this man and the others like him? Has he kept quiet enough in his bitch of a life? Has he bent his back long enough? And if there are — there always are — famous and unctuous wise men to say that all is for the best in the best of worlds, in the name of the North, the South, the East and the West, so be it.

And the Brothers, of whom I am, of whom I don't deserve to be but of whom I am all the same, by the pity of the Virgin Mary and the protection of a few men who have loved me, and whom I have sometimes, bitter as it was to me, had to combat, have the Brothers been silent enough? Have they kept their mouths shut long enough? All that must now be brought out. All that will be expressed, without anger, whatever the timorous think, without rancour, whatever the imbeciles think. All that must be expressed serenely, which does not mean mildly.

I repeat that I am not unhappy. I have to keep saying it, for they would like to make me out a snarling puppy, a malcontent, a frustrated climber. I renounced all power a long time ago. I renounced money. I renounced human love. (Enough, enough, my little blue rabbit, don't get carried away. Take a long breath. Nobody is asking you to exhibit your holy wounds. Everybody knows you've renounced heaps of things. You had nothing and you renounced it all, everybody knows that.) I am not unhappy, I am the way I am. I make a fuss because I don't want my people to miss the boat. We mustn't miss the boat, we're far enough behind anyhow.

I have one more explanation to make. I never get through making explanations and explaining the explanations, so thickly is the field mined. A joker asked me one day, "Are you a Catholic or just a Brother?" I am a

Catholic. I would not live five minutes outside the Roman Catholic Church.

Take note that it is very little to say, "I am a Catholic." Any politician or businessman will call himself a Catholic. What does that mean? It means that in this Province Catholicism still pays, financially, politically, and socially.

Then, I am a Catholic. I stick to all the formal teachings of the Church. Where a variety of opinions is authorized, I explore with the lantern I have, without pretension, holding very lightly to the little to which I do hold.

I have already said that I dismiss in advance apprentice anticlericals who would like to use my testimony (it is far too easy to be anticlerical in the Province of Quebec) along with the timid devotees and the sanctimonious fanatics. I'm not telling anybody anything he doesn't know already, but sometimes it's a good thing to yell. "I had never been aware before," says Mauriac, "how rare it is for a man to think out loud, or how formidable. He says nothing but what he sees, and he sees nothing but what is in plain sight. But the very evidence of what he points out makes him a man to be feared."

I shrink from pious verbal explanation — words like apostolate, vocation, and the like scare me a little. It is so easy to hide behind piety. Nevertheless I will say this much, that my only purpose in writing is to serve the Church.

And so goodbye.

APPENDIX

THE LANGUAGE THAT WE SPEAK
(*Le Devoir*, October 21, 1959)

I've just learned from television that our spoken language gets better and better, that our teachers are doing their best, that various competitions stimulate the universal zeal, that the school commissioners put the question on the order of the day, that the children set themselves to work with the best will in the world, that our families themselves....

All that was said in one mouthful.

It really astonished me.

I have four children in school, several nephews and nieces, and their friends. Among the lot of them, they attend about twenty schools. Exceptions, I imagine, because among ours practically every one of them talks joual. Do I need to explain what joual is? Their parents know very well, so let us not scandalize the others.

It takes hold of them the moment they enter school. Even before that, it penetrates little by little, by osmosis, as the older ones gaily bring the good news home. The boys are the worst; linguistically they wear their black leather jackets. Everything gets by, the swallowed syllables, the vocabulary cut short or expanded, always with the same result, the limping phrases, the manly vulgarity, the raucous voice trying to be tough. But the girls are catching up. A conversation among young adolescents resembles guttural yapping. From nearby it becomes more harmonious but incomprehensible. Their language has no consonants except some special ones that go click-clack. And sometimes at the end of the year they bring you a prize for good language. It's enough to make your toes curl.

The fathers and mothers I know all grumble. They must be the parents of the unfortunate exceptions. I even know some who send their offspring to English schools. Do you know why? Because there the children will not pick up "that frightful accent." That's very intelligent and respectful. For one is sure not to mangle French when one learns only English. So the language will die, but it will die virgin and martyr.

I find we have too many exceptions. Let then these admirable children who perfect an admirable language at an admirable school appear before us. Let them be produced; I want to meet the results of the good language competitions.

The disintegration which the spoken language of French Canada is undergoing is enough to frighten anybody. A few individuals make progress, but the average keeps going down. Most of the children at a certain age reacquire something like the language they hear at home; often that is no great accomplishment. They arrive at an idiom compared to which the soap operas have their charms.

Am I cherishing an illusion? It seems to me we used to speak better, not so slurred, not so coarse, not so screechy, not so Joual. But who will settle that? When the universities get their millions, they will be able to commission linguists to conduct an inquiry on the state of our language. Maybe then we shall learn how so many good intentions can bring about such pitiful results.

André LAURENDEAU

Enjoyed BROTHER ANONYMOUS ?

Now read his autobiography, the sequel to this volume :

FOR PITY'S SAKE : THE RETURN OF BROTHER ANONYMOUS